Praise for *Conversations That Connect*:

This is a book for practitioners written by someone who is a practitioner. Brooke's passion for customer care is crystal clear. She takes time to show you her point of view and how to emulate what she believes. If you want to learn how to create a customer care program that is strategic and empathetic, this book is for you!

—**KATIE ROBBERT** • CEO, Trust Insights

No matter what your industry is, marketers aim to meet customers where they are, and 'where they are' is on social media. But it was hard to convince executive leadership that investing in a social-led customer care strategy would pay off—Conversations That Connect *will help you do that.*

—**JILL SAMMONS** • Senior Vice President of Marketing & Strategic Communications, BCU

Praise for Brooke B. Sellas:

Brooke's perspectives have continuously inspired us to rethink how we approach both our social media campaigns and the potential of social media itself.

—**TEQUIA BURT** • Editor-in-Chief, LinkedIn Marketing Solutions Blog

Brooke has been on the leading edge of thinking differently about how social interaction impacts a business' bottom line. The insights and practical applications she outlines here are a must-read for any business trying to make their social media strategy more comprehensive and impactful.

—**LUKE REYNEBEAU** • Vice President of Marketing, Sales Assembly

CONVERSATIONS THAT CONNECT

How to Connect, Converse, and Convert Through Social Media Listening and Social-Led Customer Care

BROOKE B. SELLAS
Foreword by Goldie Chan, CEO of Warm Robots

Copyright 2022 Brooke B. Sellas
All rights reserved
Printed in the United States of America
10 9 8 7 6 5 4 3 2 1

No part of this publication may be reproduced, stored in or introduced into a retrieval system, or transmitted, in any form, or by any means (electronic, mechanical, photocopying, recording, or otherwise) without the prior permission of the author. Requests for permission should be directed to brooke@bsquared.media, or mailed to Permissions, Brooke B. Sellas, B Squared Media, P.O. Box 137, Stanton, NJ 08885-0137.

The web addresses referenced in this book were live and correct at the time of the book's publication but may be subject to change.

Library of Congress Cataloging-in-Publication Data

Names: Sellas, Brooke B., author
Title: Conversations that connect: how to connect, converse, and convert through social media listening and social-led customer care/ Brooke B. Sellas.
Description: First edition. |New Jersey: B Squared Media, [2022]|
Identifiers: LCCN (print) 2022907788
ISBN (paperback) 979-8-9861685-0-0 ISBN|
(ebook) 979-8-9861685-1-7
Subjects: |Business|Psychology|

ISBN: 979-8-9861685-0-0
eISBN 979-8-9861685-1-7

This book is dedicated to my sister Lauren, who made me want things beyond myself and was the catalyst for this entire journey.

To my parents, who took me back in at twenty-nine years old and told me to do whatever it takes to pursue my dreams.

To my youngest sister Taylor, because I said so (and because I stole her straightener when I moved back home, #SorryNotSorry).

And to my husband, Alex, who has never wavered in his support for me: my constant cheerleader, my life partner, my whole heart.

Acknowledgements

This is the first book I've ever written. A lot of people held my hand. Like, a lot. Huge thanks to each and every one of you, including:

Katie Robbert, who has been my work bestie and therapist. She's a constant resource, a wealth of knowledge, and generally just one badass human. She also helped me realize an even better flywheel than we had originally created.

Jill Sammons, whose name you will see throughout this book. Her positivity is boundless, and she not only supported me with writing this book but has offered so much more in the way of friendship.

I couldn't have done this without Jamie Teasdale. I so appreciate our long conversations and all of her heartfelt feedback.

Linleigh Masters because I have the most brilliant customer experience conversations with her.

Rich Brooks, thank you for encouraging me to write this and for sharing his book and writing resources. It was very much appreciated!

Evan Hamilton and Ross Quintana, a huge thank you to both for allowing me to tap into their gifted minds and quote their genius in these pages.

And thank you so much to Kelly Santina and Zontee Hou! These ladies helped me realize exactly what I needed to round out the book, which was a foreword by Goldie Chan.

Goldie Chan. I'm so stoked that this super smart queen of CX agreed to write my foreword, thank you! Goldie is one of the most compassionate humans I know.

I'd be remiss if I didn't mention Edna Ponton, who proofread this beast. Thanks, Edna!

Robert Kovach, who became my book buddy. He shared resources and stories (and heartaches and laughs)! I'm incredibly thankful to have him as a longtime client and friend.

So much gratitude goes to Taneasha White, who made me really sit back and think about the words I use and how those words affect everyone around me. If you need a sensitivity reader for anything you're doing, Taneasha will give it to you straight (but with zero sting).

Luke Reynebeau is my rock. Not only did he help me as an early reader, he literally made my dreams come true when I asked for the most giant favor ever in the history of favors and he said yes without batting an eyelash.

Kristy Morrison! Thanks for being a ray of sunshine and a longtime team member. And obviously, many thanks for letting Coco star as a beautiful anecdote for the book!

All my friends from Sprout Social deserve a mention, but specifically to those who helped with this book and went the extra mile to develop the accompanying workbook with me: Alicia Johnston, Matilda Schieren, Justin Woods, Aisha Quas, Aubree Smith, Carly Hill, Heliz Mazouri, Jade Melcher, Jamia Kenan, Katie Woods, Lizz Kannenberg, Maria Jackson, Mary Keutelian, Michelle Grano, Mike Blight, Ronnie Gomez, Suleen Lee, Sydney Nielsen, Veronica Krieg, and Walt Valo.

The entire social-led customer care team at B Squared Media. Each team member has such incredible talents, and so much compassion. I admire them all for running toward the Negative Nancys on the daily—and making all of this (gestures wildly) come true.

Ken Benson, for saving the day when it came to layout and making sure the book is professional as possible and follows all the rules.

Chris Wszolek, not only for formatting everything into "pretty" pages and designing all of the delightful images you'll see in this book, but for making Tanya and I cry-laugh with your sassy humor.

And Tanya Ponton. A client, turned team member, turned trusted partner, turned editor . . . I can't believe this is the culmination of our eight-year relationship. I'm incredibly lucky to have someone of your caliber help me carefully craft my words. Thank you for making me slow down and tell my story. Thank you for being my friend. If you're looking for a wordsmith wizard, you've found her. This "recovering lawyer" will challenge you in the most wonderful of ways.

And finally, a huge thanks to the many who are too vast to name—especially all of the team members, clients, and business partners (new and old) who carried the Think Conversation, Not Campaign™ torch alongside me.

Table of Contents

Foreword — 1
Introduction — 3

PART I: LEARNING TO LISTEN — 11

Chapter One: "Where Do We Start?" — 13

Chapter Two: The Social Penetration Theory — 21

Chapter Three: The Digital Customer Journey — 37

Chapter Four: Social Media Intelligence — 51

Chapter Five: Look Who's Talking—Audience and Community — 61

Chapter Six: Social Media Listening — 71

PART II: CONNECTING AND CARING — 91

Chapter Seven: Having Conversations That Connect — 93

Chapter Eight: Social-Led Customer Care — 129

Chapter Nine: A Word on Automation and Bots — 153

Chapter Ten: Coding Conversations	161
Chapter Eleven: Metrics and KPIs	175
Chapter Twelve: Teams, Not Tech	187
Chapter Thirteen: Final Feelings	199
Appendix: Resources	207
Afterword: How to Support This Book	211
Notes	215
Index	223

Foreword

During the more than fifteen years that I've worked in digital marketing, the same directive is given again and again: *"connect with our customers."* That's been true both at my agency, Warm Robots, and at various roles I've held at major startups and large companies. This was often followed by "sell" to that same audience.

Priorities have shifted as we've entered an ever-noisier digital universe. Today, we are online more than ever: both for work and social use. Yet even with this frequent internet use, in 2020, "Loneliness in America," a survey from Harvard University, revealed that more than 36 percent of Americans feel loneliness and lack of connection.

We are connecting less, yet online more.

If we are basically engaging less with each other socially, how do we think about how brands engage with their audiences? The answers are in both our intuition and the data.

Brooke Sellas has been a champion of customer care and engagement for years. Her work in the digital space speaks for itself—both in the impressive clients that she has represented as well as in the way she personally handles her social media (which is how we met). I have tapped her for my *Forbes* column "Personal Branding and Storytelling in the Digital Age" to speak succinctly about social media strategy and she has very pleasantly obliged.

Conversations That Connect is both a reflection of Brooke's warm and welcoming personality as well as her insightful and incisive views on customer care. One of my favorite parts is her discussion of

Social Penetration Theory (SPT). She explains how we can intelligently think about the way that we connect like layers of an onion, each layer revealing more intimacy and trust. Her case studies are also detailed and thoughtful.

Connect through real engagement.

With *Conversations That Connect*, Brooke gives us a charming view into how we can structure conversations that resonate and connect with our audiences as a brand, and as a person, if we wish to do so. A great read.

Goldie Chan, Founder, Warm Robots. Contributor, *Forbes* "Personal Branding and Storytelling in the Digital Age." Named "Top Voice for Social Media," *LinkedIn*.

Introduction

This story starts with a few beers (as all good stories do). They call beer a social lubricant for a reason—it's known for helping people relax in social situations. But it's not just the physical anxiety that alcohol reduces. What it really does is help you share more information about yourself. Instead of talking about the weather all night, people talk about politics or their childhood or their deepest fears. And those kinds of conversations actually make people feel connected to each other. Usually, it takes a while to get to that point, but a few beers let us slip past the small talk. We establish trust with a stranger sooner than we normally would. That trust gets us to open up and it can lead to good things. Or not! But it certainly lets us all get to know each other.

In this case, those beers didn't just start a conversation; they changed my entire professional path. But we'll get to that later. First, let me set the scene.

It's early 2007, I'm in my mid-twenties and living my best life. I'm working for the Cystic Fibrosis Foundation (CFF) in Dallas. As the director of special events, I am tasked with running twelve events that raise just under a million dollars for our chapter. One of my first big initiatives is figuring out how to get more young professionals involved with our organization through new events geared specifically toward them. Historically, CFF's donors were comprised of a much older demographic. Since cystic fibrosis only affects about 33,000 Americans, it's not as popular a charity among younger folks.

To help achieve my goal, I created a young professionals leadership committee (YPLC) and asked them what would make them *want* to get involved with an unheard-of charity. Some of the marketers reading this would call this a *community*—a group of individuals with a common cause. In this case, our group was eager to support one another with a shared goal of raising both awareness and funds for our organization (not unlike the goals of many marketers!).

This is where the beer comes in. Our YPLC decided to host a pub crawl through the streets of uptown Dallas. Attendees would form teams and "crawl" to several bars; those bars would support the CFF by giving donated or very discounted beer. In return, the bars were receiving a slew of new customers. And our group (and the CFF generally) would gain local awareness with our targeted demographic (young professionals) and raise money to support cystic fibrosis programs.

The next task was getting the word out about the event . . . and this is where my life would change forever.

Being in their early twenties, several YPLC members wanted to use Facebook to market the event. Personally, I had barely come to know about Facebook from my younger cohorts in 2006. I was still a Myspace girl (I know, I know . . .).

In early 2007, Facebook did not have business pages or advertising—that critical update would come later that year. So, we created a Facebook profile much like you'd use a Facebook business page today. We called the profile "Generation Cure." We created a logo and used it as our profile picture. Then we added each committee member to the profile. Next, we began asking all our friends to become "friends" with this profile. Again, pages didn't yet exist so instead of "followers" we were asking for "friends"! Up until this point, CFF approached fundraisers like this with a "rally the troops" marketing approach. In a traditional business context, it would be the equivalent of sales. But instead of trying to convince people to buy a product they had never heard of, we were trying to inform them about a disease they didn't know about and encourage them to donate.

Because Facebook was a social platform, we weren't really selling. We were having a conversation with friends and family (and friends of friends) about this cause that impacted us personally. Most people connected to CFF had a personal connection to cystic fibrosis (CF) and the YPLC was no different. My sister, Lauren, has CF and I had given up a lucrative career in real estate to pursue raising awareness. Many other members were equally passionate about the CFF's mission. Back then, Facebook was still almost entirely personal relationships, so our CFF profile was just an online space for other young people who cared about CFF to connect. There was no sales angle—it was just having a conversation. We didn't know it at the time, but we were building a community of people, united by a common cause.

Social media—as we now know so well—was an incredibly efficient way to build that community. In real life, each connection is one person at a time, or at best a small group. But online, those connections are visible to everyone. As we all shared our personal feelings, others not only "friended" our profile, they also began to participate in the conversation. Over the next few months, the profile caught fire. Word started to spread and eventually we had thousands of "friends" on our profile.

After three months of promoting the profile and the event, our pub crawl day arrived. We amassed a whopping 7,500 attendees. We exceeded not just our awareness goal, but also our financial goal. Average first-time events made around $5,000 at the time. We ended up grossing around $60,000—which was twelve times that! This was thanks, in part, due to social media's power of marketing to many versus traditional marketing, which is one-to-one.

What I realized was that social media allowed people to have conversations and connect—people didn't just accept the invitation to the event; they could share their own personal stories about CF (or beer!). We were creating a community, even if it was only gathering us around a one-time event. I was floored; a little seed that was planted in 2007 started to grow in ways I couldn't have imagined back then. Eventually I would revisit this experience and focus on it for my college thesis—just how and why this social phenomenon was so powerful. Later, it would be a huge part of how I approached building my digital marketing company, B Squared Media. And even today that experience is incredibly relevant—the foundation of how to approach the (much evolved) world of social media in the business context, which led me to writing this book today.

By pure happenstance, our Facebook profile for a (nonprofit) business purpose was just months ahead of the curve, in early 2007. Facebook introduced business pages later that year, in November. But it didn't take long for brands to realize the stunning power of social media marketing. By 2021, advertising revenue on Facebook's business pages was $117 billion.[1] (By the way, that's roughly the size of the entire U.S. beer industry). Fifteen years (and one pandemic) later, Facebook business pages are not only established; they are a massive business.

Here's another thing that happened. As Facebook business pages and advertising took off, business page followers (the "community") began to use those pages as a forum to discuss the business. Like our pub crawl, people didn't just follow the business pages—they began to have conversations and form a community to discuss their experience with the brand. And by discuss, I mean complain. A lot. These days, people use social media to go on absolute tirades when their delivery is late, or their shirt arrives without a button. (Let's just call it slightly overreacting, with "slightly" being optional.) The emotions are high!

Brands look at this feedback on their products and services with equal passion, aware of the impact it has on current and potential customers. I believe that most brands really want to be responsive to this feedback. Unfortunately, social media is a twenty-four seven conversation, and few businesses can participate at all hours. These public complaints always seem to come about an hour after the company's customer support has left for the weekend. The team comes back Monday morning after the nasty tear-down has been out there without a response for two days. That's a real problem because consumers expect a response on social media in thirty minutes or less, including nights and weekends.[2] Now the brand has two problems. One, you've already blown through customer expectations and experience regarding that missing button. Two, your delayed response to the complaint. Ouch. For a company that's trying to get their arms around the massive potential—but also vulnerability—of this relationship with their community, it's formidable. By the time brands come to B Squared Media to help with this problem, they are overwhelmed and agitated. The single biggest question we get from clients is some form of:

"Where do we start?"

The problem is twofold, and so is the answer. First, brands need to understand why those buttons are breaking. We call the online customer experience the digital customer journey. And I think of each of those negative points in that journey as "potholes": you want to turn those negative moments into wins. Social media exposes your broken buttons to the world, but it also gives you a platform to announce when you've fixed them.

Second, responding to your customers in a timely way is part art, part science. Ideally, you would find ways to not leave them hanging all weekend! But when you do respond, you'll need to do so in a way that feels authentic and personalized. In fact, most of your contact with your consumers on social media needs to be that way. Even after all these years, social media platforms are ultimately more social, and less sales-y. The pub crawl community felt connected because people shared feelings and opinions. And businesses must do that as well. But they're not. They're relying on facts, or worse, clichés—pushing traditional style content marketing in a digital conversational space.

When brands participate in the conversations happening around their industry, their brand, and their competitors on social media, we call that "customer care." It's *not* about pushing content. It *is* about building connections. And coincidentally (or maybe not), it's one of the *only* strategies that both acquires and retains customers.

Let me say that again. Having the right, non-shallow, non-cliché conversations on social media can not only help you retain the customers you do have, but it can also help you acquire new ones as well. Conversations help you make emotional connections and build communities. So, finding the potholes along your customers' digital journey is critical. Sure, we need to work hard post-purchase to retain good customers along the journey, but we also need to make the road smoother and more inviting for those deciding whether or not to take it.

Who This Book Is For

This book is for business leaders who want to learn from the work, data, and studies my agency and I have run for middle market and enterprise brands across a hugely diverse range of industries. This isn't for those who just want theories . . . it's for leaders who want to see how it works—really works—in the real world. It's intended for marketing leaders, chief marketing officers, social media and marketing directors, customer support teams, product marketing teams, and generally data-driven business leaders who see the value in using social media channels for connecting with new customers and building trust and loyalty with existing ones. It doesn't matter if you've never used social media listening or tried social-led customer care. I'll walk through the foundational steps of doing those things. For those who are already leading the charge with those types of social media activities, I'll offer case studies and data for building even bigger initiatives. If you use, like, and stand behind social media marketing, this book is for you. If you're striving to be a more customer-centric company, this book is definitely for you!

While all are welcome, this book only lightly touches on social media 101 fundamentals. So, if you're looking to learn how to use social media, this is probably a book for down the road when you're using social media channels more comfortably. So read on ... but only if you dare.

How This Book Is Organized

In Part I, I'll answer that critical question: "where do we start?" I'll explain why and how most brands are failing to capture loyalty because they're living in a reactive state of using social media for growth—even after two years of pandemic life has moved everyone online, including onto social media. I'll show you how the social penetration theory (obviously named by psychologists and not marketers!) is key to those connections—why sharing feelings and opinions will help you build brand loyalty. We'll unpack how gathering social media intelligence and using social listening can take you from that reactive state to a more proactive one. I'll also explain to you why brands are missing a key ingredient to connecting with their communities—having conversations that connect.

In Part II, I'll help you start having these conversations—not just listening but building relationships. And I'll give you the tactical, practical "how-to" advice most books leave out. We're talking in-the-trenches, straight from the streets, real-life examples that will show you the power of conversations that connect. I'll explain how the most important of these conversations happen during what I call social-led customer care. We'll talk about how to find the right metrics to measure your results. And we'll even discuss how to build the right teams or integrate a professional partner if you need outside support.

So, let's get started.

PART I
LEARNING TO LISTEN

CHAPTER ONE
"Where Do We Start?"

"Where do we start?" As I said in the Introduction, the most common question I get from clients is "where do we start?" They're simply overwhelmed by the demands of caring for their online audiences. They get caught up in which platform to use, how to get people to connect with them, how to manage those conversations, and how to deal with the (very public) complaints that people post online. It's a lot, and I get that! And I hate to say it, but brands are failing at this. Customers have been unhappy with brands for quite some time. And when the pandemic pushed nearly all of us online, they took their complaints with them, and posted them all over social media.

Consumerism in Crisis

First, consumerism in general is, and has been, in crisis for years. Most customers are looking for improvements to the most fundamental elements of a business relationship:

- concern that a brand will overpromise and underdeliver (trust)
- wary that a brand's squeaky-clean image is dark and dingy underneath (transparency)
- tired of cliché content that feels like more noise; just fluff and regurgitation; replication and redundancy (value)
- customer experience that feels commoditized, not personalized (recognition)

These are the same basic tenets of a personal relationship. And like a personal relationship, people want to be recognized. Of the problems listed previously, recognition is one of the biggest missing pieces brands are facing; *customers want personalized conversations with brands.* They want to be recognized as individuals, not dollar signs. Yes, some companies now "see" us—using our name, tracking our preferences—but are they really investing in our feelings? Or are they just counting clicks?

An important part of the solution to resolving this crisis is brands must completely revisit how they converse with consumers on social media. Very few brands are using social media to build authentic relationships, though they may think they are doing so. I see marketers using the words "communities" and "stories," but they aren't engaging in storytelling that leads to the conversations which truly connect them to communities (current and would-be consumers) and build loyalty. Many brands view connection as gaining a "follower" or a subscriber. But it's more than that. Connection is a two-way street; it requires reciprocity.

Authentic conversations are becoming the heart of what counts as a good customer experience (CX), and if customers don't feel good about their experience, they will switch to another brand, because with online shopping it's easier than ever. And everyone is online. Which brings me to the new pain point—the pandemic. If the crisis in consumerism is the wound, then the pandemic is the salt.

Since March 2020, the onset of COVID-19 and related crises have taken an emotional toll on consumers in the United States. A survey by *Forrester Research* sheds light on what's needed to ease consumers' distrust and vulnerability.[1] This book is being written in the shadow of the pandemic, but I think that you'll see these fundamentals—which were really in place long before the pandemic—will remain in place long after COVID-19 is gone. *Forrester's* report encourages brand marketers to focus on the following three areas (and I'll remind you throughout this book!):

1. **You must know and use consumer emotion in your messaging, product, and experience.** Consumer emotions are the

key to catalyzing economic and social recovery. The high levels of consumer energy in this moment reveal that consumers are enthusiastic and open to new brands, products, and experiences. However, the lurking threat of coronavirus variants, hesitation around vaccine compliance, and residual fear or trauma from the crises of 2020 mean that the consumer psyche is still fragile. Chief marketing officers (CMOs) who connect with consumers in an emotionally intelligent, empathetic way can allay lingering consumer fears and encourage excitement and optimism for the road ahead.
2. **Tighten community bonds.** Over a third of online adults in the U.S. say they are spending more time thinking about how they can play a role in their local community, and many consumers are projecting this motivation onto their brand choices. As consumers compensate for months of isolation by finding their community groups, allow your brand to be the great connector that brings like-minded consumers together.
3. **Prove your brand promise more urgently than before.** The confluence of social, cultural, and economic disruptions is creating a path for businesses to step forward as some of the most trusted entities. Consumers, employees, and partners are desperate for businesses to promise safe and secure relationships; consumer energy shows that customers are giving brands permission to play a bigger role in their well-being. Now is the time for companies to embrace trust as a strategic imperative before competitive players lock in consumer trust capital first.[2]

The Pandemic Pushed Us: We're All Online Now

None of us were prepared for COVID-19—but in particular, we couldn't foresee how the pandemic would accelerate online consumerism, including social media usage. Many analysts believe that the pandemic pulled forward the rate of online interactions by at least three years and in some industries, by as many as ten years. A 2021 McKinsey study found that on average, 80 percent of customer interactions were online.[3] But up until now, most brands used digital transformation primarily to drive cost savings, not customer experience, and certainly not brand loyalty.

Except, in today's environment, customer experience and customer loyalty are becoming the drivers of digital transformation. Why? Because everyone is shopping online. Everyone is talking about brands on social media. And they're talking *with* brands on social media. And those conversations are becoming the customer experience. Remember in the introduction when I talked about those broken button complaints? On social media, those conversations become the customer experience. Brands must become adept at those conversations. It's not just cost savings—it's brand awareness, customer support, and loyalty . . . basically, the whole ball game.

And this trend toward higher levels of social media transactions will transcend the pandemic. At the time I'm writing this book, we've spent over two years dealing with the effects of COVID-19. We've formed new online shopping and social media habits. We're unlikely to go back to "what was." From now on, there is essentially no barrier to switching brands. Customer experience and customer loyalty are defined by their online experience. Brands that can't meet these customers' needs where they are, and connect in ways that are personalized and authentic, will lose them to someone who can. It sounds scary because it is.

Figure 1-1 shows how COVID-19 accelerated digitalization of consumer interactions—by several years![4] In 2019, only 36 percent of customer interactions worldwide were digital, by July 2020, it was 58 percent.

Yet even with the stakes as high as these, companies are still mostly reactive. They have been playing catch up since the beginning.

Figure 1-1

Average share of customer interactions that are digital (%)

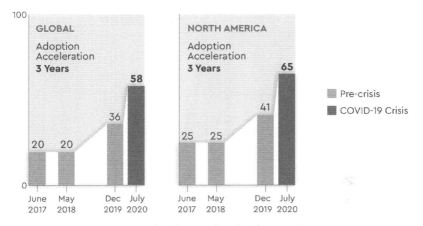

Source: B Squared Media. Based on data from McKinsey & Co.

They're chasing the latest social media platform, instead of being focused on the consumers, and they're pushing content (because they are chasing purchases) instead of building communities. If you have the right kinds of conversations and build a digital customer journey that delivers a stunning customer experience, you will build loyalty. And that loyalty creates advocates for your brand who in turn sing your praises on social media—leading to more new customers. This kind of self-propelling momentum is part of the digital customer journey flywheel, which we'll discuss a bit later.

Ultimately, social media provides power to consumers by allowing them to control their own digital journey. But it means companies also have a new power—they are not limited just to being reactive when there are issues because their consumers can proactively reach out to them via any channel at any time with questions or concerns. The opportunity to understand what your customer is thinking to fix this crisis is paramount. Using social media data allows you to provide them with a responsive and personalized experience. The importance of social media comes from its potential for gathering insights about how your customers are feeling (which we call social media intelligence), and then using that information to refine their digital customer journey toward connection, conversation, and conversion. And the ability to not only know what they do and don't like, but correct it, and broadcast it, on social media is kind of a new superpower. With well-executed social-led customer care (managing your consumer audience via social media), negative feedback is your friend.

Social-Led Customer Care: You Can't Be a Nine-to-Five Brand in a Twenty-Four Seven World

In 2020, one of our clients, a billion-dollar technology brand, presented us with this scenario: they were simply unable to handle the influx of customer service complaints via their social media platforms on time, let alone address the positive comments (yes, you need to respond to those too—more on that in a bit). They were in the same boat that most corporations are in—your employees work roughly nine to five, Monday through Friday. But as we know, social media never sleeps. So how are brands and "regular" employees supposed to be responsive to customers in a twenty-four seven world?

That's another question I hear constantly. What I've learned, dealing with all kinds of organizations, is that negative criticism is a beautiful catalyst for change. Give me *all* the bad . . . it's so telling. But you also have to look at the positive, the audience as a whole and know your customers' digital journey inside and out. We agreed to partner with this client to help them be as responsive as possible, help them learn how to connect to their audience with real conversations on social media, and leverage that negative (and positive) feedback into an improved CX. We call this social-led customer care. It is *not* just customer support—traditional help lines dedicated solely to solving problems of existing customers—it is everything from starting conversations with those who barely know the brand, to problem solving for unhappy customers, to engaging with satisfied customers who can become advocates.

B Squared Media had already beta tested this social-led customer care concept for almost two years, working with an enterprise brand in the luxury appliance industry. We kept perfecting how to triage brand conversations and mentions, how to build out paint-by-numbers internal processes and documentation for solving client situations, how and when to automate, what had to be escalated, and metrics to measure success. (All things I plan to lay out for you in this book, by the way!)

Armed with all this information, we officially launched our program with this enterprise technology brand. Within six months, we had *improved response times by 3,278%*—from more than twenty hours to under fifteen minutes! We also increased their response volume. Initially, the client was only able to handle an average of fifty-six complaints per month. Six months after partnering with our team we were handling 1248 complaints per month—that's a 2229% increase. I know these numbers sound insane—they were to us too in those early days!—but we quickly realized that the fundamental structure of organizations and the need to manage social media-based customer support simply were an inherent mismatch. A professional partner that could be responsive seven days a week, 365 days a year—and implement a robust experience-driven program designed for the needs of this space—quickly made an enormous impact. It was a shock to me, and sometimes it still is.

But we also provided so much more—we were able to not just solve an unhappy client's problem on Saturday nights, we were able to identify opportunities for the company to pre-emptively remove problems (what I will refer to as "potholes" later) from the customer experience. And we helped them create a CX so satisfying that their users began having conversations about their products—showcasing online how they used them personally. We were delighted, but not surprised. I knew the experience of that pub crawl on Facebook was hardly a fluke!

CHAPTER TWO
The Social Penetration Theory

Before I was able to help billion-dollar brands connect with their communities on social media, I had to get back to that beer. I was still fascinated by how and why the CFF pub crawl Facebook community developed as much as it did. Remember—we raised *twelve times* what a typical first-time event does!

I left the Cystic Fibrosis Foundation and found myself back in school, now a communications major at Penn State. It was 2009, and I was working on my undergraduate thesis, which was a study of the social penetration theory. (Let's call it SPT for short.) The SPT looks at how we form deep, trusting relationships. The two social psychologists who formed this theory said that "as relationships develop, interpersonal communication moves from relatively shallow, non-intimate levels to deeper, more intimate ones."[1] For my study, I wanted to understand if the SPT, which was formulated in the 1970s, still applied today and in a much different medium. Specifically—can brands use the social penetration theory to build relationships through social media? I wondered if it was similar to how we do so in person—or in real life (IRL, as we now often refer to it)?

Social Penetration Theory: The Four Degrees of Self-Disclosure

Social psychologists Irwin Altman and Dalmas Taylor created the social penetration theory as a way to describe how relationships are formed through different degrees of self-disclosure.[2] Self-disclosure is the process of deliberately revealing information about oneself that is significant and would not normally be known by others.³ Self-disclosure is a central concept in the SPT—and something I want to focus on—because this is the critical area where many brands are missing out. Altman and Taylor claim that by gradually revealing emotions and experiences, and listening to their reciprocal sharing, people gain a greater understanding of each other and display trust.

Breadth and depth. Self-disclosure has two aspects: breadth and depth. In the beginning, people often share a lot of superficial information about themselves (breadth), while more personal topics are considered "off-limits" (depth). In most cases, when first getting to know each other, people only disclose "safe" details about themselves, such as their music tastes, mainstream hobbies, and interests. As we build trust and understanding, depth increases, gradually moving to revealing more intimate details, such as religious and political beliefs, personal values, and opinions or feelings—often about more difficult experiences. This process of peeling back layers to reveal ourselves is why the SPT is also called the "onion theory," as illustrated in figure 2-1.⁴

Altman and Taylor's hypothesis stated that the way we form relationships is by disclosing information to one another. Ultimately, those disclosures lead to trust, which deepens relationships. As we progress through levels of disclosure, each stage becomes more revealing than the one before. Naturally, the more time we spend with others, the more likely we are to self-disclose more intimate details about ourselves. According to the SPT, there are four types of information that we share.

Clichés. The first type of information is clichés, which are regular, everyday responses we provide in social settings. They can be used to acknowledge someone's presence, are usually considered causal, and do not qualify as self-disclosure. It's not personal; it doesn't even have to be altogether true. For example, when someone asks, "How are you?" and you respond "Fine, thanks." (Even if you're not fine at all!) Think: casual elevator encounter, talking about the weather.

Figure 2-1

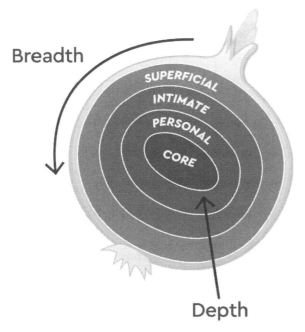

Peeling the Onion

Breadth

SUPERFICIAL
INTIMATE
PERSONAL
CORE

Depth

Source: B Squared Media, based on Altman and Taylor's theory.

Facts. The second type of information is facts. Facts must fit the criteria of being intentional, significant, and not otherwise known. But there's no real vulnerability yet; we're not at a trust-building stage. They may or may not count as disclosure, because disclosing important information suggests a level of trust and commitment to the other person, which signals a desire to move the relationship to a new level.[5] For example, my real name is Jennifer Brooke Sellas, but I've gone by Brooke since birth. That's an interesting fact. I know it's interesting because I often hear about it when people see my legal name somewhere. ("You're Jennifer?! I had no idea!") Indeed, facts can be less than boring and even interesting. But you must make the effort to make them engaging: "my name is Brooke Sellas" won't cut it.

Opinions. Opinions, which are the third type of information, are more revealing than facts. Opinions expose more information about oneself. A fact is an objective truth; an opinion means it's true for you. "It's raining" is a fact; "rain is depressing" is an opinion. While facts can be compelling, they're often not that revealing. Telling people my real name is Jennifer is interesting, but still relatively impersonal (if the DMV knows, it's probably not much of a secret). But if I said, "I lived in Texas for twenty-nine years. I now call New Jersey my home. I don't think people from New Jersey are as rude as they're made out to be (but the people who engineered going right through a jug handle for a left-hand turn need to lose a lot of cool points), or that Texans are dumb just because they speak slowly."

Those are my opinions—and you may not agree. If you don't, we might not have too much more to say to each other (especially if you defend the jug handle). But if you do, we are likely to deepen the relationship and reach the holy grail—feelings.

Feelings. The fourth and final type of information we self-disclose is feelings. This is the deepest level of disclosure as the communicator is revealing more about how they feel—which in turn creates a clearer picture of how your relationship might develop.[6] Emotional, as opposed to factual, disclosures are particularly important for boosting empathy and building trust. Compare the Brooke example in the facts section, with this version which uses feelings: "I am eclectic; I can listen to Frank Sinatra and Deadmau5 during one car ride and feel exhilarated and invigorated by both. I believe in energy, in karma. My happiness is based on the happiness of those who support and surround me; I keep my circle tight. I hate that we can't be a more open-minded society, but love that we have the freedom to decide what we want to believe and whom we want to love."

In those few sentences I shared far more feelings. You probably felt something or some way about what I said. Maybe it was bad.

Maybe you laughed. Maybe we have something in common. In any case, I disclosed a pretty good amount about who I am, and you probably decided in a minute or two whether I aligned with your own values. That's the power of words that go beyond clichés and facts. And it can be done in just a few sentences!

SPT works online the same way as in real life

It's worth pointing out that the original SPT was established in the 1970s, way before we were all online. But, the role of establishing trust in a partner (or audience) before revealing more intimate information is also supported by the "boom and bust" phenomenon in online relationships, described by psychologists Alvin Cooper and Leda Sportolari in 1997.[7] With online interactions, they found that anonymity gave participants a sense of security and made them disclose personal information much earlier in relationships than they would face-to-face, making relationships exciting and intense ("boom"). However, when the necessary trust foundation has not been established, the intensity of the relationship can be impossible to sustain, leading to dissolution ("bust").

So, there was evidence that the SPT didn't only apply to in-person relationships, but even when we build them online. But did that extend to relationships between brands and consumers online, specifically via social media? This question was the basis of my thesis in college. The answer was not only mind-blowing for me, but it also became the foundation of my career and ultimately my company.

Social Penetration Theory and Brands

My thesis asked this question: Based on the fundamental assumptions of SPT are brands doing enough with their social media content to reveal a "personality" that people identify with and want to form a relationship with? Because the psychology behind the SPT says that by disclosing information about yourself (or your brand) to other persons (your community, customers, or would-be customers), you will prompt reciprocity with some of your members, thus creating trust, and ultimately, a relationship.

As I conducted my study, I looked at how brands (nonprofits specifically) used social media content and conversations on Facebook to build trust with their community and customers. It's too bad that beer couldn't be used as a social lubricant for my study participants, because the majority of the results were pretty abysmal! All three of the non-profit brands I followed during my study spent much of their time on cliché content, meaning it lacked originality or was tired and overused. This kind of content and conversation does not lead to trust, relationships, and loyalty.

The graphs in figure 2-2 represent some of my thesis work on the social penetration theory.[8] However, you can easily see that the deeper, more intimate levels of communication were not happening—two of the three had content that was more than 50 percent clichés! And these are non-profits! You'd think they would be the model example of how to elicit deeper feelings and opinions from their audiences. After all, they are asking people to give money out of a sense of goodwill, not in exchange for a product or service.

I graduated in May 2011, with distinction (Penn State's way of saying "with honors") thanks to my undergraduate thesis work. I was even invited to the Pennsylvania State Capitol to share my findings with other selected students of our class to participate in the Eighth Semi-Annual Undergraduate Research at the Capitol—a poster conference showcasing outstanding and award-winning projects by undergraduate students from Pennsylvania.

Think Conversation, Not Campaign™

With that thesis work in my head, I was struck by the idea that what most organizations were inherently doing wrong in the early days

Figure 2-2

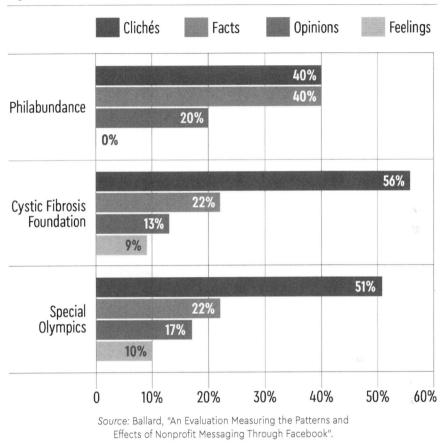

Source: Ballard, "An Evaluation Measuring the Patterns and Effects of Nonprofit Messaging Through Facebook".

of social media was putting an emphasis on pushing out content. They were thinking in the traditional terms of marketing campaigns, not building relationships on social media through conversation. The idea "think conversation, not campaign" came to me. I was so struck by it—and downright protective of this—that I even deleted it at the last minute from a speech I was giving to the National Bowling Association (yes, really) before I started my own company because I wanted to keep this idea to myself. Soon after, I trademarked it.

A year later, in 2012, I founded B Squared Media, a boutique, social first, digital marketing agency. Our tagline became—you guessed it—Think Conversation, Not Campaign™.

For those of you reading this book, you should apply the same concepts of the SPT to what your brand shares through social media content. Remember, people aren't following your brand on social media because they "like" you, it's because they want to get to know you. That "like" can grow or dissipate based on your self-disclosures and how they align with ideals and values of the groups of people who follow you. That means you should focus on the breadth your audience needs to build relationships first. Once established, you can proceed to deeper levels of self-disclosure. The SPT suggests this as well, based on the levels or types of disclosures we share to build trust. Let's look again at the four stages of disclosures, but now connecting the SPT to online conversations between brands and their audiences.

Clichés: the kryptonite of content. This is essentially non-disclosure, and whether you're an individual or a brand, the problem is the same. Clichés don't reveal anything personal, nothing about the core values or brand's personality. Clichés are what many companies and brands deem "appropriate" content. It's certainly safe; but it's also uninspiring. And with the excess of mundane content, this level will hardly beckon people to connect with you or your brand. There's nothing wrong with the occasional cliché (see fig. 2-3 for an example from ProFlowers of one that works), but I urge you to limit clichés to no more than ten percent of your total content.[9]

Facts: make them fun, not flat. As I said before, facts are true but not necessarily revealing. For a brand, this can be the company name, product price, hours of operation. When brands rely on facts, I call this purgatory because it's where many of you get stuck. You've got those casual relationships but almost no disclosures. You're not building a connection. There may be an audience, and they may be reading every post (best case scenario). But since the brand isn't

Figure 2-3

Clichés are ok. But use them sparingly!

Source: Proflowers (@ProFlowers), Twitter.

sharing anything, they aren't either, so you certainly aren't building trust. While you (the brand) may be moderately showing who you are, you aren't really going there with true transparency ... so you're not gaining it, either. Again, it's not offensive, but it's also not memorable. Look at the example in figure 2-4 from United Airlines.[10] The audience that looks at this might fly, they might not. They might choose United ... but probably not because they feel connected to them. There's nothing personal from this brand in this post that

Figure 2-4

This post ran in the New York/New Jersey market. *In winter.* **This picture just begs for a better tagline, right?!**

Source: United Airlines (@united), Facebook.

connects them to the audience. There's information, but no emotion. We'll talk more about how to make facts more compelling than this, but you can see the inherent risk when you stay at this level of disclosure.

Own your opinions. This is when you begin to reveal your brand's character, what your brand beliefs are. There is vulnerability at this stage because your audiences may or may not like you. Or, as I mentioned earlier, it's less about liking you and more about finding out that your values don't align with theirs. If they dislike your revelations or values, they might back away, or retreat to a less vulnerable level. But if they agree with your brand's opinions, then they will be more likely to move to level four, feelings. Truly authentic brands start to emerge when they share their opinions. The opinions don't have to be radical or controversial to connect: in figure 2-5, Pro-Flowers takes a stance on flower species.[11]

Feelings connect your followers. When you get to the feelings level, the brand and its audiences share how they feel about things; this is when we're most vulnerable, and therefore, we assume that trust has now been established. As a human, you know that you can trust someone a little, or a lot. You earn it, and you can lose it. It's no different for brands and their consumer audiences online. At this stage, there is a more even exchange of psychographics—feelings, opinions, beliefs, attitudes, values—from both the audience and the

Figure 2-5

I mean, I guess the carnation controversy is a real thing, but this opinion feels pretty safe.

Source: Proflowers (@Proflowers), Twitter.

brand. Two-way conversation has emerged. Your brand's feelings can (and should) resonate with your audience, but they don't have to be about a topic that is in the news or deeply personal. The goal is to connect with your audience by revealing what your organization's values are, the personality and culture of the brand, or just an emotional articulation of why you provide the product or service that you do.

In figure 2-6, you can see how Sharpie (the pen people) created this downright provocative tweet that is full of feelings, but mostly just amusing once you realize it's about a pen.[12] I hope you can see why feelings are so key to creating connections. It doesn't matter which platform you are on, or even what you sell. The way to set yourself apart is to be authentic and interesting and memorable.

Your brand and the SPT

Take a moment to pause here. Ask yourself these questions: Where does our marketing sit based on our level of disclosures? How is our brand revealing itself? Is our messaging, content, and culture going beyond breadth and going into depth? Again, I get how terrifying this can be. The most innocent reference or comment can produce backlash from your audiences. This is especially true when the conversation participants have little prior history with your brand. Which leads me to urge you to make sure you know who you're talking to at each stage of your brand's digital customer journey (we'll get more into that soon).

Different conversations are needed at different times and will be better served in different media or to different groups (or "segments" as we marketers call them). But even at the risk of ... taking a risk ... I say, "nothing ventured, nothing gained." How are you going to discover the nuanced values of each one of your target segments if you don't share similar information? Yes, self-disclosure involves risk. But it can also lead to extraordinary results.

Figure 2-6

Uh, they're talking about a pen, folks. . . .

Source: Sharpie (@Sharpie, Twitter).

If now you aren't too pleased with your content and conversations—don't worry! That's the whole point of this book. So, stay with me.

By the way, none of this happens overnight. It takes time and energy for your audiences to engage with you. What's key is that you are doing it—giving out just as much, if not more, of what you are asking. All in all, the SPT follows a well-recognized pattern of the "greater the ratio of rewards to costs, the more rapid the penetration process."[13] Your audience segments are constantly trying to weigh the potential outcome of interacting with you on a reward versus cost scale. This reward-to-cost ratio suggests that you can build relationships faster when there are positive self-disclosure experiences that bring people through the stages and into deeper disclosures (on both sides).

This is what my thesis revealed. If brands want to attract and keep (acquire and retain!) customers through social media, there's nothing better than using content as a cornerstone to build an environment where potential and current customers can have a conversation with your company—as well as with each other. Additionally, the kinds of messages (content) that received the most supporter responses in my study were—you guessed it—the ones that sought out opinions and feelings. Furthermore, posts that used storytelling (or "soliciting stories or narratives" as I called it in my thesis), produced the deepest-level disclosures, or opinions and feelings.

My findings were that the SPT applies to brands and consumers today, even with social media as the medium. We haven't changed the way we build relationships: vulnerability → trust → intimacy.

Based on my thesis, and a lot of real-world experiences with clients, I'm convinced that this applies to brands. If you were to share more content about your brand's values—including sharing and asking for opinions and feelings—what do you think would happen? My belief is that your brand would gain more closely aligned audience members and lose those who are not as agreeable with your values.

In SPT, this is referred to as "de-penetration" or "dissolution"—and it shouldn't be seen as a bad thing. This is what the smartest of brands do; they want to shed the lurkers and followers who aren't active and won't turn into purchasers, all the while gaining more of an audience who will move from connection → conversation → conversion. It's. So. Beautiful. Right?!

Limitations of the social penetration theory. Of course, as with all "magic" marketing things, including cool social psychology theories, I feel compelled to tell you both what the SPT does for us as brands and where it may fail in being 100 percent adequate in explaining the formation of all types of relationships.

For one, the SPT takes a nomothetic approach. A nomothetic approach means studying numbers and statistics to draw universal conclusions. Some say an idiographic approach would be better because that method emphasizes the subjective and unique experience of an individual. I'm sure I don't have to tell you that people are *huge* variables.

Second, by claiming that deeper self-disclosures will ultimately lead to greater relationship satisfaction, the SPT ignores many other factors that can influence relationships. For example, it doesn't recognize the vast range of cultural practices and personalities that exist on our planet. Furthermore, the social penetration theory was developed based on research in a Western, individualist culture (United States). Self-disclosure may not be a requirement for successful relationships in all cultures, meaning the SPT could be culturally biased. Therefore, the SPT has limitations, and if your brand markets to an audience in a culture that has different values and norms, it may not be appropriate.

SPT helps drive digital transformation

Finally, how we establish relationships via emotions and feelings in this new era has significant differences from the past. Brands must build relationships using social media (and other media), while still leveraging the principles of the social penetration theory. The SPT has always applied to brands and consumers but now must be executed in new ways because of digital transformation. The media we use have changed. The conversation is more digital (in particular, on social media) than analog, and more conversational than direct advertising.

But it's *not* about which platform you're using. It's also *not* about content itself; it's about using content in a way that joins people, which then should lead to conversations that connect and convert.

As I mentioned before, this is especially true now because consumers are so disjointed and disrupted. Not only due to the explosion of technology, but even since the pandemic started, our habits have vastly changed. The need to connect to others who share our values is more important than ever. And so is knowing *whom* to connect with.

But, of course, using the social penetration theory to connect means understanding when and how to have these conversations in this new era. How do you bring a 1970s social theory onto a 21st century platform? You need to know where your online audiences are, starting with when and how they interact with you. These days, consumers are using all digital platforms (websites, email, SMS) to connect, as well as social media. They use them all to discover your brand, learn about you, and (hopefully) purchase from you. Therefore, it's critical that you fully understand your consumers' digital customer journey. Which we'll talk about next.

CHAPTER THREE
The Digital Customer Journey

Many of you know the growth flywheel model from Jim Collins' book *Good to Great*.[1] The central idea of the flywheel is that your customers are your best salespeople. If you make your customers happy, they'll tell their friends. If you make your product or service easy to learn about and easy to purchase, those friends will also buy it. And they will tell their friends, and so on. Basically, like a flywheel, the momentum builds off its own energy.

Flywheels have largely replaced traditional sales funnels because a funnel suggests that people enter at the top as visitors (or strangers) and exit the bottom as paying customers. But consumer purchasing habits have changed significantly. Today, consumers don't necessarily enter the funnel at the top and go down in a straight line to purchase. They can enter from the side: for example, they might be the end user of a product but not the purchaser (you receive a beautiful bouquet of flowers and then begin to use their service yourself). Or from the bottom—for example, with freemium models where you are a user of the product or service long before you upgrade and become a paying customer. And because the customer experience is now online, and often includes social media, a brand builds customer loyalty with great social-led customer care, a concept we will discuss fully later. At B Squared Media, we updated the flywheel to take these new dynamics into consideration.

The Digital Customer Journey Flywheel

As you can see in figure 3-1, we modified Collins' flywheel to reflect the more symbiotic relationship of community, connections, conversations, and conversions. You can see that we have put "customer care" in the center, which reflects the customer-centric philosophy that we, and most of our clients, subscribe to. (Collins' version had "growth" in the center.) By putting customer care in the center of the flywheel, we're focusing our efforts on conversation-driven elements of social media that still follow the traditional model of "attract, engage, and delight."

However, we're building brand strength by taking it a step further and looking at how to do those things through community, connections, conversations, and conversions with a holistic approach. Each of these areas work together to drive the momentum that creates a stellar customer experience. But what I really think you should focus

Figure 3-1

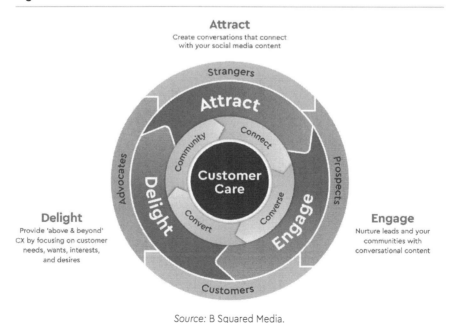

Source: B Squared Media.

on is that in this flywheel *customer care touches all stages of the digital customer journey*. A flywheel is about creating momentum—and done right, customer care is the extra push into overdrive. They are the most impactful part of your organization because they're interacting with your audience, customers, and community and feeding that social media intelligence to your marketing team, your sales team, your product development folks—all the way up to your C-suite.

Customer care is comprehensive. Customer care is much more expansive than traditional customer support (sometimes referred to as customer service) help desks. Customer care at first glance might function like traditional customer support ... but only because brands are treating it that way. When you have customer care in the social media context, those conversations can—and absolutely should—do much more than just solve an immediate problem. They can answer a question like "how do I change the cartridge in my printer?" But users don't interact with brands on social media in such a siloed way. Expect—and be prepared to answer—a wide range of questions. For example, "Does your printer have smart technology compatible with Alexa?" is a sales question. (We'll talk later about the acquisition potential in social-led customer care—you'll want to take note, trust me!) Your customer care team should be able to answer that too. Further, they could even tweet or post that information if lots of people were asking them. ("Did you know you can operate our printer using Alexa? Here's how.")

Traditionally, brands have a sales team, a help desk, and a marketing department—all separate from each other. But a social-led customer care team can be (and should be) all those things—attracting, engaging, and delighting. Since it's online, the questions they are being asked can be—and should be—analyzed and that data distributed to all departments. Again, we're going to get into all of this later, but I want you to note that social-led customer care should be integral to business decisions across the organization. Maybe your research and development (R&D) department needs to ensure that the next model printer is smart. Maybe your marketing department needs to make that information more prominent on the packaging. We'll get into all of this in more detail, but the important point of our updated flywheel is that it's using social-led customer care to recognize the power of customer-centric business, and that customer care creates momentum from these customer interactions that inform all aspects of the business.

The digital customer journey (DCJ) is the experience a person has with your company online from before they buy, to during their decision to make the purchase, and then post-purchase. You can think of it as every potential interaction that would-be and current customers could have with your brand along their digital journey. Perhaps the first time your potential customer sees your brand is through an online ad. Or maybe one of their friends recommended your product and shared a link to your website on their Facebook page. Those are both interactions with your brand on their digital customer journey.

We use the flywheel to illustrate how the momentum of the different stages can expand your community—deliver a good CX to a new customer, then delight them, and they will tell others online, attracting your next customer. But to deliver a superior CX, you need to understand at a more granular level each stage of the journey. These days the customer journey is nonlinear so you won't always know which point will turn out to be most critical.

The Digital Customer Journey Stages

You should start with identifying the digital touchpoints at each stage of the journey, and then learn to listen to the conversations being had around each of those touchpoints. And then eventually, you'll be ready to have conversations at each point. All the information you are gathering is part of your social media intelligence, which we'll discuss in Chapter Four: Social Media Intelligence. But to gather this information from social media sites, you must first become intimately familiar with your customers' digital journey, and each stage, which you can see in figure 3-2.

Let's go through each stage of that journey:

Awareness. Awareness is where your potential customer realizes they need something they don't currently have. Maybe their oven broke, or they've decided they want to buy a bike. And what do we do

Figure 3-2

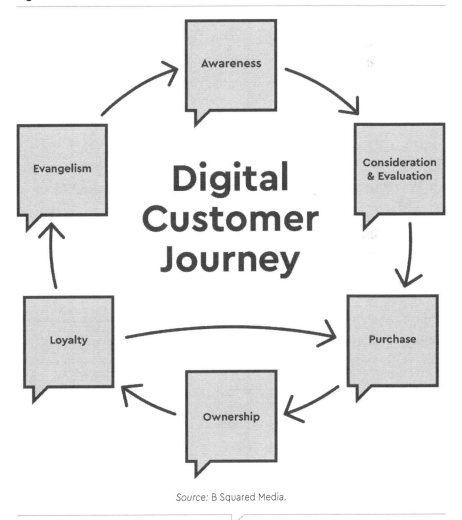

Source: B Squared Media.

when we need something new? We research. We turn to the internet and ask questions of our peers on social media. Note that I didn't say we go to the brand itself for our research—we might, but consumers often trust others' interpretations and opinions (via social media and elsewhere) rather than the brand itself (or its official resellers) to help us decide. That's different from the days when you would walk into Best Buy and ask for help choosing a television. So, when your brand does have the opportunity to interact with consumers at the awareness stage, it should be ready to engage in these direct or indirect conversations, the right way, at the right time. You're not trying to hard sell anyone (I hope!), but you are there to provide content that helps with awareness, like answering frequently asked questions (FAQs), or offering tutorials, spec sheets, and blog posts.

Consideration and evaluation. After the consumer has done their research, they're likely to evaluate their short list of potential options. At this stage, they're looking at the brand's product reviews, watching product videos, or asking for demos. Budget is an important part of consideration, too. Price sheets are likely sought out at this stage. From the brand side, you'll want to ensure you have content that helps you set your brand apart from others. Differentiation and responsiveness are key at this stage.

Purchase. Obviously, this is the stage that most brands focus on, for good reason. With more and more purchases happening online, this phase has become extremely important in the digital customer journey. Here are examples of where you want to check for problems: Can your customers easily create an account (or log into their existing one) and add items to their shopping cart? Are there options for upselling or cross-selling, without being annoying? Is it difficult to apply discounts or purchases using a digital wallet? These are the kinds of things that are critical to a smooth digital journey and customer experience.

Ownership. Ownership is what happens right after purchase. At this stage, your key goal is retention. This is where the customer is evaluating a different element of CX: the post-purchase experience. For example, how well was their order fulfilled, including shipping and delivery, as well as online, real-time tracking. It also entails all your post-purchase support, such as online customer support, and the quality of your support content (for example, FAQs, instructions, and assembly guides). And don't forget things like support chatbots and assisted chat, follow-up emails, and social media interactions. Many people skip ownership/retention and go straight to loyalty—but you can see what an extremely critical role CX plays in this stage alone.

Loyalty. This stage is about creating loyalty, and it comes in all shapes and sizes: loyalty programs, personalized rewards, customer newsletters, public or private communities, and social media-led customer support. But an even bigger factor in creating loyalty is establishing an emotional connection with your customer. This is one of those key moments that brands often don't capitalize on—building an authentic conversation with owners (customers). This is when you should be checking on the relationship and finding opportunities to strengthen it. The questions to ask yourself include: Are our customers feeling good about us? Are they receiving the value they expect from the brand . . . at every touchpoint? Does that include their social media exchanges with the brand?

Most brands know it's easier to keep a current customer than to gain a new one. But does your investment in your social media marketing (and ideally, social-led customer care, which we'll discuss in Chapter Eight: Social-Led Customer Care) reflect how important this stage is? These customers are your past and your future. As you saw in the digital customer journey diagram (fig. 3-2), there's a line between purchase and loyalty. That's because a happy customer is a repeat customer. Your goal is for them to stay in this loop: purchase, happy (loyal), purchase again.

Evangelism. If you have repeat customers and are able to turn them into a mouthpiece for your brand's marketing and advertising goals—that's evangelism. (By the way, some people refer to this as advocacy—or, from a paid partner perspective—influencer marketing.) Since consumers want to buy products from businesses they can trust, they often turn to their friends for recommendations. Brand or product "evangelism" helps brands build their trustworthy reputation and creates word-of-mouth recommendations. This is key, because what today's evangelists say about your brand becomes part of the information that new would-be customers read during their awareness stage. Therefore, the journey should be thought of as a circular path, not a straight road. Getting members of your community to the evangelism stage today is tough. Most brands can hardly maintain loyalty. But if you can build this community, you can benefit from an almost organic momentum of evangelical customers bringing in new customers.

Understanding potholes

As you go through each stage, you want to be on the lookout for any potholes on that journey. We're not looking for best in class, luxury level experience on this journey—we're just looking for an absence of bumps. What do I mean about potholes in the digital customer journey? Let me use a real road to explain.

The main problem with the road to Maine. My husband and I vacation in Maine during the summer. Our little summer cottage sits on a big hillside overlooking the Atlantic. The views are stunning, you feel as if you're on the edge of nowhere, and it's peaceful. We and our small handful of neighbors all love that it's remote. Part of that remoteness means that you must travel down a very rough dirt road to get there. You can't even see the ocean as you're driving; it's just this narrow, one-lane road through a thick forest of pine trees. Most of the houses in our thirty-two-home association have been passed down generation to generation, so people have been driving over those potholes for decades. Our little dirt road is a point of contention at every association meeting. Everyone complains about the potholes on our dirt road, because sometimes they can be bad enough to be a concern. However, no one expects the perfect smoothness of a modern paved road. They just want a very nice dirt road! The neighbors, young and old alike, want the road to be level enough to not be a distraction when driving down each summer with their extended family in tow.

You've got to pave your DCJ. This is the same with people looking to buy from your brand. They just want their digital journey to be smooth. To use another traveling metaphor, people often say the best flights are the boring ones. The journey should be without turbulence or other drama. Most people think about social media data generally, but to answer, "where do we start," I tell clients to begin with where *your* bumps are in the digital customer journey. There are often potholes on a road, but as a business owner or leader, your job is to find them and resolve them.

The potholes reveal themselves through negative data—where your users are having negative experiences in their digital customer journey. Social media intelligence allows you to observe where your potholes may exist. In my experience, marketers like to gloss over the negative parts. You've got to stop doing that. You'll see me argue that one of the best things you can do is just the opposite—run to the negative—that's where you should put a lot of your energy.

Go back through the DCJ again, this time checking for potholes. Notice the points I made in the purchase stage, for example. You don't want anything to deter them: issues with their digital wallet, inability to see shipping times, whatever. Once the bumps in your digital customer journey are identified, ask yourself *why* do those potholes exist? Specifically, why are people giving certain points in the road a bad review, or even leaving your brand altogether? How can you smooth out the road? It's not easy (or pretty!).

It's a dirt road. Not a red carpet. People tend to think of the best customer experience as "rolling out the red carpet": a huge fanfare. This leads to CMOs and marketing leaders thinking how they can give their customers a parade down the entire road, which immediately feels scary and not scalable. But CX is about finding those potholes and fixing them, so the journey is smoother and more pleasant. Remember, you just want the journey to be easy.

Digital Touchpoints

Consider the variety of digital touchpoints you have—or should have—with consumers when creating your own digital customer journey, and along the way, make sure to check for potholes. Your goal is to optimize the customer experience by making sure users have what's needed to communicate with you, no matter which digital channel they choose. You can start with your existing digital touchpoints to help you understand where you are having the most interaction. Get very specific and track each channel and what kind of interactions you're having. Let's look at some examples of where you might start:

Your website. Which pages are people clicking (specific products? online manuals?)? How long are they staying on the page—one report says the average time a customer stays on a page is fifty-four seconds—how do you measure up?[2] What about other interactions: Are they chatting with live agents or a chatbot? What kinds of questions are asked most often?

Emails. What are the click through rates on your emails? Do they vary by time of day you send them out? Which sections are clicked? Do people respond to factual news like new product announcements or sales, or do they like anecdotes about other customers using your products?

Your website and email are just a couple to start with: don't forget customer feedback on third party sites (online reviews and similar), SMS marketing (text messages), and paid advertising.

Social media. We're going to spend tons of time on your social media digital touchpoints in particular. Partly because the kinds of

information you get on social media are wildly more robust than digital channels like websites and email. You can see individual responses, as well as responses to that response (depending on the channel and privacy settings). Here are questions to consider:
- Which channels get the most interaction?
- When do people respond?
- Do they ask questions? Make complaints? Showcase their own use of the product?
- Which kinds of interactions get additional participation (likes or follows on posts or retweets)?

One of the benefits of social media is that you can also get much more information about who is saying what. Website and email data mostly tells you how many clicks you got, but not from who. Social media lets you see (again, subject to the channel and user restrictions) who is saying it, where they are. It's data on data on data. (In fact, so much data is a challenge with social media intelligence. But we'll talk later about how to narrow your lens to what really is useful for you.)

Don't stop at your current channels. Find out where you ought to be. You can create surveys for new and existing customers to pinpoint the digital channels they most prefer. If you know the demographic of your target audience (which you probably do) you can use that as a basis to help you determine how to reach them. Baby Boomers prefer different channels than Gen Z—know where your audience is.

Look at others' social media channels. Another huge advantage of social media is that you're not limited to your own channels, you can see others' as well. We'll get into tagging and tracking conversations that don't tag (@mention) your brand specifically later. But you can find out how your audience becomes aware of your brand—and it's possibly not on any of your social media channels. In figure 3-3, paint brand Sherwin-Williams clearly follows multiple interior designers on Instagram. This makes a ton of sense—how often have

Figure 3-3

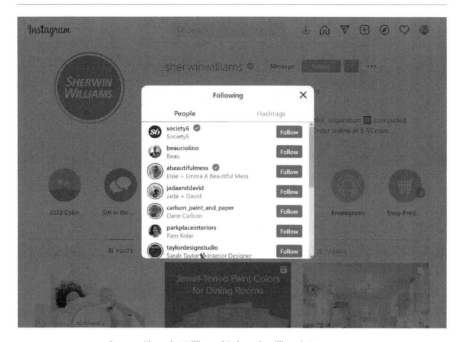

Source: Sherwin-Williams (@sherwinwilliams), Instagram.

you looked at a home design social media page and then chosen a paint color, as opposed to starting with the paint company's website? For some brands, your own social media channels won't be the place where your audience goes through the awareness and consideration stages of the DCJ.

Finally, ask yourself the following questions when it comes to your digital touchpoints:

1. Who interacts with the touchpoints you've identified: customers or potential customers?
2. Which types of interactions do the touchpoints entice from users: requests, complaints, or positive feedback?

3. What comes next—regarding touchpoints—in the DCJ? How can you determine what triggers each stage of the journey?
4. Lastly, you'll need to plan for who will own each touchpoint. For example, who is interacting with the user at each digital touchpoint? Someone from marketing? Your customer support agent? A bot?

Testing your digital customer journey. Once you have a digital journey created, it's time to test! If you need buy-in from the C-suite, explain the test as "quantifying customer purchasing behaviors online." Tell them that by understanding the touchpoints of a customer's digital journey you will be able to eventually reduce customer complaints, increase loyalty, improve the e-commerce experience, and discover opportunities for new products and services. That should get their attention.

For each stage of the journey you've created, analyze the following data sets:

1. **Outcomes.** Which actions did users take during each stage of your journey? Examples include customer acquisition or support questions on social media, live chat questions (acquisition or retention), email support asks, downloading content, chatter or conversation, etc.
2. **Pain Points.** Next, describe what users were feeling at each touchpoint. Are there areas of your digital journey that are creating friction? For example, maybe you have long wait times for a reply on social media, your email responses are delayed over the weekend, or your bot can only provide limited support for difficult asks.
3. **Iterations.** Understand what's working now as well as what's not . . . and how to improve. Make iterations as needed.
4. **Rinse and repeat.** Continue to refine your digital customer journey over time. We recommend updating continuously

with anecdotal and metric-based insights to quantify what your gut says about your journey.

You will almost certainly see that you have a lot of touchpoints and will soon start gathering a lot of data at each of those points. All that data is what builds your social media intelligence. I believe this should be the lifeblood of your customer care strategy, informing who to reach out to, when to do it, and what to say when you do.

CHAPTER FOUR
Social Media Intelligence

One of the key things we'll talk about is social media intelligence—using and understanding the data that you can glean from your social media channels. When we talk about social media intelligence, we're referring to all the solutions and tools a company might use to analyze and respond to online conversations and social signals, as well as analyzing those social data points into anecdotal evidence, based on the voice of the customer. Social media intelligence allows those who use it to gather data in ways that are both non-intrusive (data from conversations with no participation) and intrusive (data from conversations with participation).

Social Media: The Most Important Part of the DCJ

I talk about the *digital* customer journey because the online CX includes everything from email newsletters to website visits to social media. And all the data collection from each of those touchpoints gives valuable information. It can be incredibly useful to know things like email open rates and website click throughs. But they can be quite limited—you won't know *why* they opened that email or clicked on your site, only when and what sections.

On the other hand, social media data—as opposed to online data more generally—is where brands need to start investing their focus. First, so many of us are using social media more and more. As you can see in figure 4-1, during the first year of the pandemic, social media usage absolutely skyrocketed—71 percent of consumers

Figure 4-1

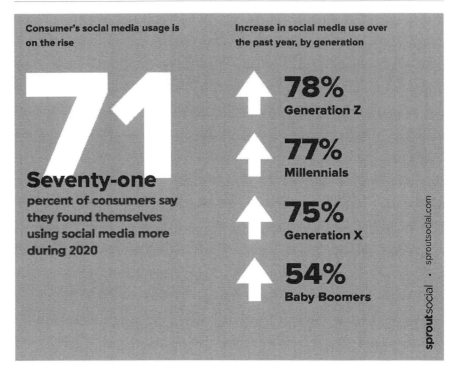

Source: Sprout Social.

overall used more social media in 2020—and more than 75 percent for Gen X, Millennials, and Gen Z, specifically.[1]

Social media is quickly overtaking email as consumers' preferred channel for sharing feedback as you can see in figure 4-2 (31 percent prefer social media versus 18 percent prefer email).[2]

Social media is also the preferred channel for reaching out to customer service (see fig. 4-3) which shows that 33 percent prefer social media, while 23 percent would rather use email.[3] Company websites, though also an online channel, fare even worse as a preferred channel.

Figure 4-2

Consumers' preferred channel for sharing feedback about a product or service

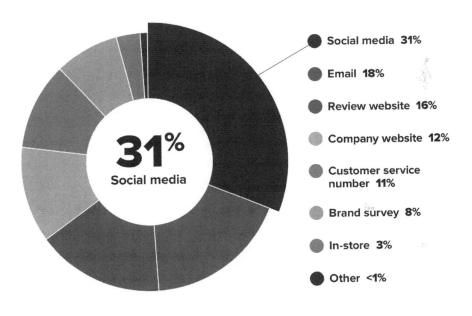

Source: Sprout Social.

In 2021, nearly 78 percent of consumers agreed that social media is the fastest and most direct way to connect with a brand.[4] And companies they label as "best in class" brands are those that are responsive, which includes good customer support and engaging with their audiences. Over and over, we've seen that these are the brands that people want to connect with.

Figure 4-3

Consumers' preferred channel for reaching out with a customer service issue or question

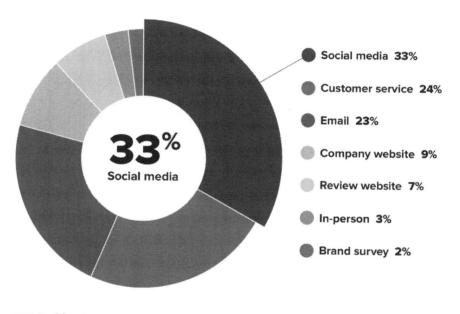

- Social media **33%**
- Customer service **24%**
- Email **23%**
- Company website **9%**
- Review website **7%**
- In-person **3%**
- Brand survey **2%**

33% Social media

sproutsocial · Sprout Social Index™   sproutsocial.com/index

Source: Sprout Social.

Email is still king ... for now. The primary communication channel for consumers is still email. That should come as no surprise. It was one of the first digital channels and is simple in nature. However, social media is moving in on email quickly. It not only integrates with email but allows brands to nurture massive audiences.

Social media is also an exceptionally useful channel for engagement. Furthermore, younger generations are more apt to use it as a primary communication channel. Social media also allows the entire customer journey to take place on one medium. From discovery to decision, and then as a loyal customer, consumers can do all the things through social media with a brand they like and trust.

I think the biggest reason that social media will overtake email as the primary communication channel is the fact that it gives marketers access to information that email can't: customer feedback, industry trends, and competitive intelligence. Each of those areas provides deep knowledge for all departments, not just marketing. My prediction is that *social media will be the primary communication channel* for consumers and brands by 2024.

Social media is also a great place for marketing research because people often post their thoughts publicly. This means you can get feedback from nearly all parts of the globe, touching a huge variety of people. It provides an array of social data around customers' conversations, preferences, and purchasing habits. In today's highly disruptive marketing space, it's important to know more than just demographics like customers' age, gender, and income level. Knowing their needs, motivations, challenges, and desires is imperative if you want to provide them with great products and services. It's also key to personalizing your interactions with them, which generally improves CX and brand loyalty (we'll discuss this in detail later).

Challenges of Social Media Intelligence

But getting a strong grasp on social media intelligence isn't as easy as looking at the data provided out of the box by Facebook, Twitter, or any of your native social media channels. And it's about to get harder—because Cookiepocalypse is coming.

Cookiepocalypse: the death of easy access to social media intelligence. When it comes to collecting and managing online intelligence, we must mention that (cue scary music) the cookie apocalypse is coming. If you've been living under a rock, the "cookie-pocalypse" is the death of the third-party cookie by Google. At the time of this writing, Google says they will be eliminating third-party cookies by 2023.[5]

This will deal a major blow to those who advertise because third-party cookies are little snippets of code that track users (or their device, technically) across different websites. Most commonly, third-party cookies are used for ad retargeting and behavioral advertising—which is largely how most brands achieve personalization for their audiences.

When Google eliminates support for third-party cookies, it could limit the number of ways marketers can target and advertise to users across the web. You need to prepare for this impending change in available data by becoming better at gathering your own customer information. This includes the ability to collect your own first-party data, some of which you can glean from social media intelligence. This will be key to surviving marketing in the coming years. The path to first-party data is building first-party relationships.

The pandemic increased the reliability of online purchasing, leading to lower brand loyalty. But one thing remains certain: customer loyalty is critical for businesses that want to stay afloat. And what do you need to win loyalty now? More personalization, which often relies on the use of cookies. Cookiepocalypse will make it harder than ever to create a stellar customer experience.

Due to the huge increase in social media intelligence, there are also new challenges to dissecting data. First, there are *so* many channels—more than 100 social media channels at the time of this writing. Second, consumers seek out information and engage with brands as they see fit, as opposed to the brand directing them. Next, it's just too much data for one person to analyze, so you must distinguish information that is available, but not useful, for your purposes. Finally, there are tools to help with analysis, but they aren't necessarily compatible enough to "talk" to each other and give a truly comprehensive view.

By the way . . . it's totally okay if you've been doing it wrong. Seriously, this is the best time to start doing this correctly. Because even if you've been diligently tracking social media intelligence over the last five years, it's probably been rendered close to useless over the course of the pandemic. Anything before March 2020 is too old to be reliable. The pandemic has shifted consumers and their behavior so drastically that data before the pandemic has become irrelevant. We've been forced to lead a digital-first life, and this current digital transformation is wreaking havoc on social media baselines and behaviors.

Less Content, More Conversation

Brands understand the importance of social media and online communities, but they don't approach those communities through a customer-centric lens. They prioritize content, not conversations; they focus on the latest platform, not the relationship with their brand's community.

Much of what brands do on social media is reactive. And that's okay. When you respond to messages, comments, or questions from your audience, that's reactive. Most customer outreach on digital touchpoints is reactive because they are often a one-off interaction with your brand. But if brands truly want to succeed on social media, they must also think of how to be proactive with their social media efforts. And very few brands are doing this well: using social media to build authentic relationships (though they pretend to be doing so). They have been playing catch up since the beginning. They still are not focusing on the consumers and chasing purchases instead of building communities.

You don't have to be on fifteen social channels, but you need to be responsive on the three you use. The point is not which channel you use. The point is that social media is where consumers are making shopping decisions now and you need robust and accurate social media intelligence to meet them there. In fact, it's worth discussing this issue about platforms a bit further.

The platform isn't the point. I've had so many clients—and even respected colleagues in this space—who put way too much emphasis on which social platform to use. We often call this "shiny object syndrome." And many of you reading this are sick with the symptoms. It seems like every other week there's a new platform (SnapChat, TikTok, Clubhouse, etc.). Yes, these platforms roll out quickly and are rapidly adopted by would-be consumers. And several platforms have emerged as not only very popular, but also enduring. Many of them—most of them—are at best hot for as long as it took you to read this sentence. Getting good at this is not specific to a platform, it's about learning to engage with your audience—and that will apply equally on whichever platform they approach you.

Social media intelligence is about understanding the digital journey touchpoints you offer, which and how often your community uses them and making sure they have a "pothole-free" experience while using them. That's true no matter which platform you're on. If you can learn to be more proactive in this space, more fluent in how to listen in on important conversations, and then participate smartly, you'll be building know-how that can translate to any platform. Seriously. I urge you to stop chasing the latest platform! Instead, invest in getting better at this skillset: at having deeper, more meaningful conversations to better define your brand and build more loyal communities. With the right connections and conversations, the conversions will come.

The Consumer Is in Control

Ultimately, social media provides power to consumers by allowing them to control their own digital journey. It also means companies are not limited to just being reactive when there are issues because their consumers can proactively reach out to them via any channel at any time with questions or concerns. The ability to understand what your customer is thinking to fix this crisis is paramount. Social media data allows you to provide them with a truly valuable experience. The importance of social media comes from its potential for gathering insights about how your customers are feeling, and then using that information to nudge their journey toward connection, conversation, and conversion.

Now that you understand the importance of the digital customer journey, and have begun to identify digital touchpoints, you need to figure out who to listen to. Yes, you know when they connect (which stage of the DCJ) and how they connect (which touchpoints). But who are they, and which ones matter most? You need to understand who your audience is.

CHAPTER FIVE
Look Who's Talking— Audience and Community

Understanding who is talking about your brand is one of the most important things you can do. First, you need to identify who you should listen to. Next, you'll need to segment that larger group into those that matter most, and why. (By the way, it's not as simple as customers and prospects, though those two groups are key.) In traditional marketing, you direct the conversation. But in social media, a lot of the conversation isn't directed by the brand. It doesn't even involve the brand. That's a radical shift of social media marketing, and it's part of why so much content pushed out by the brand is falling on deaf ears. People no longer rely solely on brand-owned content to learn about products and services. As you looked at your digital customer journey, I am sure you discovered places where users relied on other sources. You can't have good conversations if you're not listening to the right people in the right places. And you can't begin those conversations unless you are making connections. Your audience is those people who are connected to you.

So, who is your audience? What are online communities? Where do customers fit in? And who should you care about? These are important questions, so let's break it down. And many thanks to my friend and colleague Evan Hamilton, who is Director of Community & Customer Experience at Reddit and had some great insight on how to think about this: "First, we need to understand that gatherings of people live on a spectrum, from audience to fandom to community. There's nothing inherently wrong with any point along that spectrum, but they require different levels of investment and create different outputs."[1] Evan provided the following thoughts on two specific segments discussing your brand, audiences and fandoms:

> **Audience.** The most common grouping of people in the business world is an *audience*. These are people who are listening to you—subscribed to your social media channels, getting your email newsletter, reading your book, etc. These people aren't (generally) interacting with each other. Yes, there may be some interactions, but few would describe the main benefit as connection. They're listening to *you*. This is the easiest group to build, though the hardest to drive action from.
>
> **Fandom.** A fandom can look like a community, but it's not quite. This is a group of people coming together to get each other excited about something. This could be a group of music fans in an audience headbanging, or Marvel acolytes lining up for hours for a premier. This, largely, is "web3." This group is harder to build than an audience—people have to feel truly passionate—but still easier than a community. You can generally drive this group to do simple things—buy the latest record, dance, etc.—but not complex ones.[2]

By the way, most brands won't have a fandom, or won't need to leverage them. The exceptions that come to mind immediately are sports brands, music brands (the "Beyhive" for Beyoncé or "Swifties" for Taylor Swift) and brands like Apple (because they have ferocious fans—just a quirk of the brand).

Community. In the context of this book, I'm referring to online or digital communities. Building a brand community has been a popular topic as of late. Brands want their community to showcase brand loyalty to other potential customers. They want people to share opinions and feelings; they want their brand community to be emotionally invested. Because when your community is emotionally invested, they will buy from your company, engage with your content, rave about your brand to their friends and family, and more. The chance to connect directly with your devoted customers is huge—I totally understand the appeal.

Marketers *should* want to build actual brand communities to increase trust and relationships. But community is what a lot of marketers get wrong—they're using "community" as a buzzword when they're really talking about audiences. Another trusted friend and colleague, Ross Quintana, CEO at Social Magnets, said this about community: "Many people think followers are the same as a community. This is not true; followers are connections, and those connections can create a community but only if they are targeted and relevant. Most brands' social media audiences are built by simply putting out content and hoping people follow your profile . . ."[3]

As I mentioned earlier, Evan Hamilton is Director of Community at Reddit, which is basically one of the largest communities on the globe! So, he knows a thing or two about this. And he said the following: "A community . . . is a group of people with a common interest, mission, or situation coming together to interact with each other and creating more value (for themselves and for your business) through those interactions. A community would be those Marvel fans getting together after the movie to build cosplay outfits together. Or people from [a] concert creating their own band. A community is users of a business product meeting up to share tips and tricks. This is the hardest group to create—collaborating is harder than headbanging—but drives the most value."[4]

It's worth noting that you can also increase trust and relationships with conversations that connect, even with an audience not built by the brand. That doesn't mean I don't get behind the idea of building a community! I do. I think seeding a brand community is a great way to get those who are earlier in the digital customer journey to engage with your brand (awareness and acquisition). However, we think of community as a secondary or "stretch goal," whereas customers are the main goal. Make it easy for the people joining your community to contribute and share their knowledge, as well as use their influence to guide the community in an organic way. But it isn't easy, and it won't happen overnight. And once you build it, you'll have to keep maintaining it. You should be working hard now to seed your community with conversational content. It doesn't end at "if you build it, they will come."

Other important segments to consider. I'd also like to highlight some other groups that are key to understanding. They may be followers (part of your audience) or even part of your community. Or neither. But they can be radically important to you.

- **Customers.** Those who have purchased and are using your products. This group may or may not become part of your communities. They may not even be part of your audience. But let's be clear—you're running your business on customers, not community. So, we'll spend a lot of time discussing how to connect with them and build customer experiences that lead to brand loyalty.
- **Advocates.** Advocates are people who have some affiliation with the brand, are enthusiastic about your brand, and may direct people toward your brand. They don't have to be customers. That said, when you are looking for advocates, enthusiastic customers could be a place to start—a brand could look at who their repeat or high-value customers are and then start figuring out who among those also post a lot.
- **Employees.** Employees should be a part of your audience development, too. All too often, they are overlooked. Yet, getting their buy-in for the brand can lead to employee advocacy *and* uncovering insights they have into your brand's overall customer experience. Don't count them out.

- **Trolls.** Ah, yes. The internet trolls. Believe it or not, along with the sporadic troll who feels it necessary to make disparaging comments on your posts, you'll also have your very own band of trolls. Some will be customers (albeit *very* dissatisfied customers), some will be people simply spamming you with their own agenda, and some will be the necessary cost of building conversations with the social penetration theory (SPT)—sharing opinions and feelings. Remember in the beginning when I said you must be vulnerable? Well, sometimes you're going to get rejected—trolls are one type of rejection. In fact, they are such a social media pest that it's worth discussing them a bit more.

A Note on Trolls

Trolling is defined in the *Oxford English Dictionary* as "deliberately posting offensive or provocative online messages with the aim of upsetting someone or eliciting an angry response from them."[5] Unfortunately, this group isn't as easy as delete, hide, and block. I love how this article from *The Verge* explains that it's not as simple as saying, "don't feed the trolls":

> One of the most popular solutions that arose in online culture was, again, the mantra of "don't feed the trolls." This meant that any time a troll popped up in an online situation making inflammatory remarks, you were supposed to ignore them because responding would derail the thread and give them the attention they wanted. What no one seems to remember is it never worked, practically on any level. There was always someone who wanted to troll back in the opposite direction, someone who genuinely got offended for a personal and valid reason, or someone who wanted to try to be reasonable. Instead of solving anything, "don't feed

the trolls" became a motto for people who want to act above it all or regale us with stories about how much harder it was to troll back in their day when they had to troll uphill, both ways! But most of all, it became the mantra of how to ignore online abuse completely.

The premise of "don't feed the trolls" implies that if you ignore a troll, they will inevitably get bored or say, "Oh, you didn't nibble at my bait? Good play, sir!" and tip their cap and go on their way. Ask anyone who has dealt with persistent harassment online, especially women: this is not usually what happens. Instead, the harasser keeps pushing and pushing to get the reaction they want with even more tenacity and intensity. It's the same pattern on display in the litany of abusers and stalkers, both online and off, who escalate to more dangerous and threatening behavior when they feel like they are being ignored. In many cases, ignoring a troll can carry just as dear a price as provocation.[6]

We've had situations with our clients where their irate customers became incessant trolls, literally posting brand-bashing posts every hour, on the hour, for weeks. After it finally ended, we'd think they were gone, and nope! There they were again, back at it with even more fire than before. We couldn't block, ban, hide, or delete a paying customer! Most clients don't want to, and I agree. There are some who will complain incessantly, and you will need to respond, at least the first few times. You can ignore trolls who are simply opposed to your messaging, as opposed to lobbing a sincere complaint. For example, later we will talk about sharing feelings and opinions to have conversations that connect. Stating an opinion or feeling will alienate some of your audience, who will then turn into trolls—that's unavoidable. (But I'll explain why it's worth it.)

Some of you will disagree on the right stance to take regarding trolls. If you haven't yet had the pleasure of dealing with trolls, trust me when I say it's not *if*, it's *when*. Whatever your decision, make a plan! It's best for everyone if you set up some protocols to follow.

How to Treat Your Trolls—Our Suggestions:

- **Develop a troll policy.** Establish a policy for derogatory user comments. Clearly detail what kind of comments are allowed and what to do when they are against your policy.
- **Bring facts to the fight.** Misinformation is rampant these days. If it is misinformation being spread by trolls about your brand, fight back with facts. Apple did this when the iPhone 6 was released. Many internet users—some trolls—said the new phone would bend if you put it in your pocket. Apple fought back with facts by admitting there was an issue for some customers. With their radical candor, they were able to put out most of the fires.
- **Act quickly.** This is an area where response time is essential. We'll get into the importance of response rates more generally later, but for these purposes, just know that responding quickly is your best defense. Sometimes, your online troll is just a customer complaining. Nine times out of ten, good communication eases this. People just want to be heard ... right away.
- **Answer with empathy.** In almost any case, you can answer with empathy. I could probably write an entire book on trolls and how to best deal with them in a public setting, but instead of focusing on that, let's talk about a troll's kryptonite, which is empathy. While the human instinct is to push back when you get a mean or angry post or tweet, doing the opposite can work wonders. (If you're having a hard time with this, see the ten scripts I share with you in Chapter Eight: Social-Led Customer Care.)

- **Go silent.** In some rare cases, you *can* stop feeding the trolls. One of our clients had a customer who posted every hour, on the hour—for a month—that's more than 600 posts! (Yes, really.) This person didn't want to resolve the issue; she wanted attention. Her goal was to make us angry and create a public spectacle. Because we knew her complaints were being handled by customer support and the executives at the client company, we knew we could stop responding to her insults.
- **Make "watch for" lists.** We have a working list of trolls who like to continue trolling the brands we work for, especially the ones who can't be banned (like paying customers). Making this list and providing "if /then" content for how to deal with the people on this list can offer a sigh of relief for any newbies working on the account.

Intimately knowing your audiences and communities (even your trolls) inside and out will allow you to take bigger risks with opinions and feelings. Together, these groups are your most important asset because they represent those who may buy, those who have bought, and those who may buy again. From a gentler perspective, if you build a great CX for the people who make up your audience, community, and customers, they are likely the ones who will fiercely support and defend you against the ever-growing army of trolls that exist online.

Lurkers: Your Silent Audience

Before we move on, let me mention one more group. Notably, some of your social media followers will be lurkers—they may not ever engage with your content by leaving a reaction or starting a conversation. However, that doesn't mean those lurkers are not listening. For example, one of our healthcare brands has very low engagement rates, yet their click-through rate is extremely high—which is still a form of engagement, by the way. My assumption for this is that this client is a gastroenterologist group, and they help with things like hemorrhoids, colonoscopies, and other gastrointestinal issues. (You can see why people aren't clamoring to comment publicly.) Focusing on metrics like link clicks and social media traffic to their website is better for their audience which consists primarily of lurkers.

CHAPTER SIX
Social Media Listening

One tool that should be a part of any social media strategy is social media listening. Brands now have a huge opportunity to listen organically to consumers by both monitoring their conversations and then analyzing them. This includes any of your target audiences who use social media and other online media to converse.

Social Media Listening: The Opportunity

Marketers often confuse social media monitoring and social media listening. Social media monitoring involves tracking and responding to all the messages sent to or about your company, your products, or your services. It tells you what. This is where most companies live with their social media strategy. Unfortunately, that means that all too often, marketers are guessing at the why—because they are just monitoring and not listening. With social media *monitoring*, you're able to see the "what," but with social media *listening*, you can start to understand the "why." Social media listening tells you why by looking at where and how these conversations are happening, and what people think—and not just when people are tagging or mentioning your brand. Here are other factors worth noting regarding social media listening and the opportunities they provide:

- **Social media listening can tell us a lot.** Only in the last ten years has this been a real opportunity via social media. Think about it: We don't just log in to social media sites and browse; we give our names, our locations, our interests, and beliefs. We connect to others, and thereby, their names, demographic, and psychographic information. Consumers are composing epic ballads for marketers looking to target them—if those marketers are listening.

- **Social media listening is organic and unbiased.** Before social media, listening was restricted to methods like in-person focus groups. Whereas focus groups are based on a specified time and place, social media listening allows you to listen—and speak—to customers any time they talk about you, no matter where they are. (Well, mostly. Privacy on certain platforms can shield certain conversations.) Plus, this means your sample size can be larger and your data is probably richer. And thanks to social listening platforms (SLPs), they are easily captured. (You would not believe how long it took me to code conversations for my thesis work!)

- **It's about conversations among customers.** You now can listen in on conversations with customers and would-be customers—and there are opportunities to listen along the entire digital customer journey, including pre-purchase. These conversations deliver valuable insight into customers' wants, needs, feelings, actions, and desires. The more adept your brand becomes at listening, the more you'll also be able to predict and influence how customers will behave.

- **This kind of listening is better and more cost effective.** Traditional listening opportunities like focus groups are more expensive (time and money). And for larger companies, the perception your customers have about your brand can shift in weeks, even days. Social media listening offers real-time research, allowing marketers to spot micro trends and make micro-level shifts. In this regard, social listening can take you from a reactive position to a proactive one rather quickly.

- **Social media listening gathers more information—with greater nuance than previous consumer data collection.** Social listening avoids accuracy and reliability issues due to bias, which is a risk of methods like focus groups. For example, you might be getting pressure to find out about customer soda choices, but if 90 percent of your brand positive conversation is about your burger and 90 percent of your negative brand conversation is around your chicken sandwich, you probably need to be focusing on your chicken sandwich and forget the soda.

With social media listening, you can access and utilize industry, brand, and competitor insights for better data-driven decisions. By tracking and analyzing conversations around relevant topics to understand consumer sentiment and brand health, you'll be able to move from a reactive position to a proactive one.

Most of today's social media listening tools have automated sentiment scores, provide endless options to analyze collected data by topics, and deliver other meaningful business data points. However, your own goals for social listening will likely differ from other companies or industries. We've seen a wide range of goals from our own clients, including brand awareness, reputation management, marketing, customer service, and even influencer marketing.

A few words of caution about social media listening

Despite its advantages, I would be remiss if I didn't offer a word of caution about social listening. It has limitations that you should understand.

We're limited by the platforms themselves as to what we're allowed to listen to. Christopher Penn, my friend, and trusted analytics partner over at Trust Insights, offered this perspective on the limitations of social listening tools: "Social listening platforms vastly over index on Twitter not because it's a great social network, but because it's the last major social network that shares its data so freely. Every other platform has locked down its data to third parties, and so every influencer marketing software package and social listening software package is over-reliant on Twitter.

The challenge many marketers run into with any above-board social listening tools is that today's tools are excluded from gathering data from the largest platforms—Facebook's family of apps, LinkedIn, and TikTok as the leading examples. And no tools of any kind exist for extracting information from velvet rope social media communities, those like Discord and Slack, where conversations are completely opaque to the outside world."[1]

Social media listening and representation. Another point that Chris makes, that I want to echo, is the shortcomings of social listening and representation. There is an inherent issue to capturing information of certain groups that are less engaged on social media, and yet those groups could make up a large number of your target audience. Certain groups are less likely to be on social media, and certain types of brands are less likely to inspire conversation in a public arena like social media. The point of social media listening is to understand your audience, and you need to know the difference between when they are not talking about you, and not talking at all.

Social Media Listening: The Obligation

But it's not just about opportunity. Brands also have the obligation to listen to the conversation in this 21st century way, because they no longer can push out information to consumers and pre-customers. They can no longer broadcast "facts" and control what consumers know about the products. Consumers are speaking to each other: deciding their own facts about your brand. So, you need to be listening to these conversations, and not just speaking *at* your target audiences. If you don't, you may be taking extraordinary risks. One of our clients had an experience that perfectly illustrated this.

Know your audience: "The Girl" was a woman

In 2019, we worked with a celebrity and her new jewelry line. Her team wanted help understanding who her buyers were among her audience. They called their audience "The Girl" because—based on their research—their customers were (very young) women, aged eighteen to twenty-four. As we dug in, we soon discovered that their research consisted of their social media follower data. And it stopped there.

But just because your social media follower audience is mostly eighteen- to twenty-four-year-olds, that doesn't mean they're the ones purchasing your products. Their social media follower research showed that 49 percent of the users following the brand on social media were aged eighteen to twenty-four, as you can see in figure 6-1.

Figure 6-1

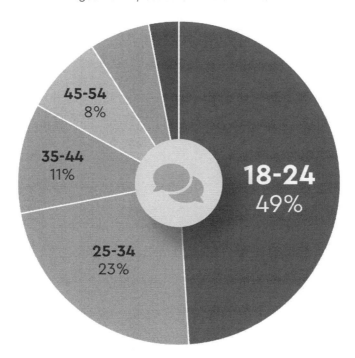

Source: B Squared Media.

However, as a part of our project, we used three data sets: social media follower data *stacked with social media listening* and "who is talking about your brand" data, stacked with advertising data that showed us purchaser information.

By looking at the full picture, we helped her team discover that 88 percent of their *purchasing* customers from social media were 24–44 years old, as you can see in figure 6-2. Only a little more than 9 percent of the purchasers were "The Girl." Yes—this brand was missing more than 90 percent of their *purchasers* by focusing only on

Figure 6-2

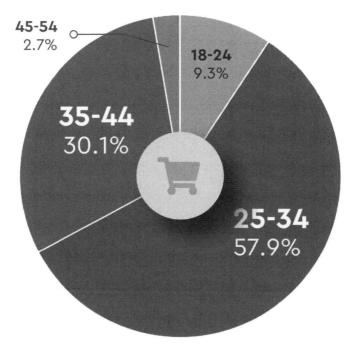

Source: B Squared Media.

follower data. What we discovered was that "The Girl" was actually "The Woman" and the brand's content needed to reflect that new understanding.

Fortunately, this case study has a happy ending because we were able to help the brand identify their actual target audience. But it also demonstrates the risks of not doing proper social listening. This brand almost created the wrong jewelry—targeting the wrong people, or at the very least, using the wrong messaging.

The stakes are high in getting your target audience right, and identifying that group takes a lot more than just looking at who seeks "customer support" or follows your brand on social media. The content marketing and messaging takeaways alone were worth the investment in a more comprehensive (and more accurate) social media analysis.

Another takeaway of this case study is that social listening, social conversations, and other purchasing data, when used together, impacts so much more than just your marketing and advertising decisions. In a second project, we helped this brand decide where their next brick-and-mortar store should be located—and that was in part based on where "The Woman"—not "The Girl"!—lived and shopped. I suggest that anyone trying to convince the C-suite to invest in social media listening explain the cost of a mistake like that.

The power of social media listening

When used correctly, social media listening answers lots of fundamental questions that brands or marketers have, including inquiries about their audiences and communications with that special group of people. I see social media as the largest "focus group" for almost any brand but without the bias of traditional focus groups. People disclose almost anything on social media, and you get to eavesdrop in on it. Not listening—or getting it wrong in the previous example—can be expensive. There is a real (actual) cost to not doing this and it will impact many levels of your business. As the jewelry case study demonstrated, it's not just a "product marketing" problem or a "customer service" problem. If you don't gather social media intelligence through social listening, you're leaving money on the table—both for pre-purchase and post-purchase stages in the digital customer journey.

Therefore, social listening is not an investment in *just* marketing or advertising; this is an investment in almost all elements of how you run your business because it involves getting to know people on a much deeper level.

Another advantage of social listening is that it helps you learn to echo your audience, literally mimicking their words and sentiments. For example, in early 2020, everyone was using the word "coronavirus." But then, consumers began referring to it as "the pandemic" or "COVID-19." We took this information to our clients midway through 2020 and told them if they were talking about COVID-19 they should mimic the words their audiences were using. This isn't as simple as semantics—when we get into conversations, we'll talk about how important it is to really hear what your customers want and how they say it. You will want your product or service to reflect their language.

Your brand messaging needs to sound like the consumer so you can build relationships and be looked upon as a peer. As humans, we learn and grow by mimicking one another, and that includes using words that others use. This type of "mirroring" helps create authenticity and allows you to be a true participant of the conversation. If we had allowed our clients who were publishing COVID-19 content to continue to use the word "coronavirus" we would have left them at a disadvantage of not mimicking what most consumers were calling it. Is that incredibly nuanced? Yes. But when you're fighting the attention war, nuance can be the difference between a win and a loss.

SLPs can help, but real listening is human. Social listening platforms (SLPs) work by mining and processing heaps of social data—and fast! Then, they think by learning (as in machine learning), clustering, and surfacing relevant themes, topics, and audience segments. SLPs are not fully autonomous just yet though. Humans are still an integral part of the social listening process—and sometimes, rolling up your sleeves and getting involved instead of delegating it all to the machines can help you learn a lot.

It's not that hard to do. Here's a quick humble brag—but with a crucial point! As you can see in figure 6-3, I was doing social listening in 2011 before there was this caliber of social listening with my thesis work![2] I was labeling (public) outgoing and incoming messages and called it a "coding scheme" to categorize both the types of messages being shared (accolades, outreach, storytelling, etc.) as

Figure 6-3

Special Olympics Coding Week 1

	11/1/2010 Totals	11/2/2010 Totals	11/3/2010 Totals	11/4/2010 Totals	11/5/2010 Totals	11/6/2010 Totals	11/7/2010 Totals
Daily Qualitative Info							
Number of entries	1	2	1	1	1	0	0
Number of responses	50	92	22	84	156	0	0
Number of "Likes" for main entry	68	165	92	467	54	0	0
Number of responses to sub-posts	0	0	0	25	0	0	0
Number of "Likes" for sub-posts	15	11	21	100	6	0	0
Foundation Messaging							
News							
Events - Past							
Events - Present							
Events - Future							
Fundraising/Soliciting Volunteers							
Issues							
Soliciting Stories or Narratives	1	1	1	1	1		
Miscellaneous		1					
Responses Content							
Accolades/Praise/Thanks	1	4	0	0	1	0	0
References	0	0	0	1	0	0	0
Outreach/Support	0	0	1	1	0	0	0
Story or Narrative	47	43	6	38	3	0	0
General Response/Statement	2	44	15	39	152	0	0
Miscellaneous	0	1	0	0	0	0	0
Depth of Disclosures							
Clichés	2	5	1	5	153	0	0
Facts	21	48	14	11	1	0	0
Opinions	19	19	2	43	0	0	0
Feelings	8	20	5	16	2	0	0
Other							
Number of Friends/People that "Like This"	92,837	92,856	92,965	93,065	93,206	93,311	93,452

While my social listening efforts were basic in 2011, they show that you don't necessarily need fancy or expensive tools to quantify relationship building on social media.

Source: Ballard, J., "An Evaluation Measuring the Patterns and Effects of Nonprofit Messaging."

well as labeling the messages as clichés, facts, opinions, or feelings. (I don't recommend using an Excel spreadsheet these days, for your own mental health.)

But my point is, this is something you can do too (and so much more easily these days). What if you used your social media listening tool to label your outgoing conversations/content with the type of disclosure it is (cliché, fact, opinion, feeling), and did the same with incoming conversations from your audiences? Wouldn't that be a cool "social media conversation thesis" of your own? We'll get to more on labeling conversations in Chapter Ten: Coding Conversations, but for now, my point is that listening requires human engagement if you're going to fully leverage it. And now that you understand the power of the SPT, try to see these conversations through that lens. What feelings and opinions are your audiences sharing? What can you share in return?

How to Listen

Listening smart takes heart. First, before we get into the fundamentals of how to listen well, allow me to get in touch with my feelings and give a bit of "woo woo" advice. If you were to take two ears and put them side by side, the shape they form looks a lot like a heart. Furthermore, the word "ear" sits right in the middle of the word "heart" (h-ear-t). The ear—listening—is the only true path to the heart. So, if you want to understand consumer behavior and drive consumer behavior, you need to learn to listen to them. Understanding is only the first part. The tactical execution of creating or guiding consumer behavior is where the real movement happens. You could, for example, pick platforms based on your customer demographics. Or you could decide to be most active where there are the largest volume of existing conversations or people discuss your brand the most. Personally, I like the second option.

How well do you know your customers' digital journey?

You'll also want to understand whom to listen to. As you saw with the celebrity jewelry brand, you'll want to make sure you're considering a multitude of factors when understanding who your audience is. Or who your community is. Or who your purchasers are.

Here's a fun exercise. Think about your customers' digital journey and ask yourself these questions:

- How do my customers move from unknown to known when it comes to our brand?
- How do my customers move from observation (like a social media follow) to participation (conversation)?
- Are we employing methods to activate our audience and/or community members through the touchpoints of our digital journey? How?
- Am I identifying advocates and influencers throughout the digital journey?
- How are we including post-purchase tactics into the digital journey, specifically for retention and loyalty?

When it comes to listening smartly, you'll have two different opportunities to listen. First, you can listen in the context of observation (reactive). Some brands find the social listening elements of monitoring and analyzing alone sufficient. Second—and ideally—you'll use listening and contributing together to improve your participation in the conversation with your audiences (proactive). We'll focus on having conversations in Part II: Connecting and Caring.

You also need to understand what listening can and can't do. For instance, Facebook privacy settings don't allow for social listening tools to scrape users' content if their profile is set to private. Also, most social listening tools don't allow you to listen in the past. Meaning, once you input your keyword and keyword phrases, the data starts getting collected from that point forward. In other words, most platforms won't let you backdate your search—at most you might be able to collect the prior thirty days (depending on the tool).

Understanding what you can and can't do, plus creating your social listening goals, will help you when you eventually participate in the conversation. For even more detail on how to do this, I recommend you get the accompanying workbook, *Social Listening Step-By-Step: How to Revolutionize the Way You Connect, Converse, and Convert* (see Appendix: Resources), which walks readers through what social listening success looks like for their brand.

Listen up: how to find your audience. One of the first things to note with conversations is whether the brand was tagged (@mentioned) when they joined the conversation.

Let's start with a simple example first, where the brand was tagged when the user mentioned them. This is your easiest listening—when the user is literally saying your name! We see a good example with Apple Music in figure 6-4.³

Figure 6-4

This is why @AppleMusic is the best!

Just saying. 😂 💁‍♂️

> TechCrunch ✓ @TechCrunch · Mar 8
> Spotify and Discord go down, forcing Tuesday upon us tcrn.ch/3J1M6rG by @jordanrcrook

2:01 PM · Mar 8, 2022 · Twitter for iPhone

Source: Jeremy Linaburg (@jeremy_linaburg), Twitter.

But you want to listen to as many relevant conversations as you can, and that means learning how to find times when your brand is discussed, even if it isn't @mentioned. Figure 6-5 is another example of a user discussing Apple Music, but the brand isn't tagged (@mentioned).[4]

Brands that are not tagged can miss these types of posts. And that can be a problem since repeat customers or even potential customers might not be tagging you. Figure 6-6 is an example where the hair care brand Moroccan Oil replied to a user even though they aren't tagged.[5] It's actually the retailer Sephora's Instagram feed, but they are clearly engaging in social listening and joined the conversation. Note here that this was a totally appropriate moment for the brand to enter the conversation as the user was specifically asking where they could find the product in another country. Sephora could

Figure 6-5

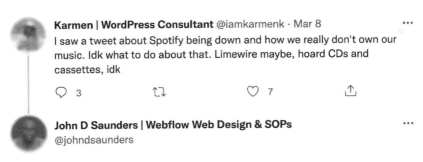

Source: John D. Saunders (@johndsaunders), Twitter.

Figure 6-6

Source: Sephora (@sephora), Instagram.

have also answered potentially, but they might not have known. So, it made sense for the brand instead of the reseller to reply.

Let's talk about what happens when your brand, products, or services are being mentioned but you're not specifically being tagged (@mentioned). This can happen for a number of reasons:

- The user attempted to tag your brand but did it incorrectly.
- The user is responding to a post of yours with another topic entirely (like needing support).
- People are talking about your products or services with each other and not intending for the brand to join the conversation.
- People are talking about your products or services with each other, and they are intending—or are indifferent to—the brand to join the conversation.

CHAPTER SIX: SOCIAL MEDIA LISTENING | 85

Obviously, if someone meant to mention your brand, you should respond. Part of what makes social listening so great is that you can "listen" for common misspellings of your company name, or product and service names. You can see in figure 6-7 an enthusiastic customer that brand Ole Henriksen might have missed, despite her best efforts to sing their praises.⁶ She repeatedly spells the brand's name "Ole Hendrickson" and because she is on someone else's channel (the beauty store Sephora, in this case), they would need to have this misspelling among their keywords to catch it. (We'll get more into

Figure 6-7

You say tomato, I say tomatah. Or, you say, Ole Hendrickson.

Source: Sephora (@Sephora), Instagram.

keywords in a moment.) Another example would be when someone comments on a post of yours—whether it's on topic or not. Even if they don't tag you, you should be listening.

The key point I want to make right now is about listening. Find your audience, even when they aren't on your channels, or even when spelling your name right! This is all preparation for when you join the conversation, which we'll discuss more in Part II. When people either don't intend for you to join the conversation, or seem indifferent—you have a choice, just listen, or participate. You can choose to enter those conversations and gently guide the conversation the way you want it to go. For example, if your company provides social listening software tools, and someone is asking for listening tool recommendations on Twitter. The person who asked the question will likely get several responses, listing several different tools. As the brand, it's perfectly okay for you to join that conversation and recommend yourself. Figure 6-8 shows an outreach example when a user asks for a social listening tool recommendation.[7] As you know by now, I'm a big fan of Sprout Social. I recommended them (and mentioned them), and they joined the conversation.

Why keywords are so key. There are broad and narrow ways you can—and should be—listening. Your social listening tool allows you to "listen" by analyzing conversations and looking for specific keywords. Keywords are the words that describe best what you want to find. For instance, on Google or social media platforms you may be searching for a brand. A keyword can be one word (e.g., "Epson"), two words (e.g., "Brother International"), many words or what we call a keyword phrase (e.g., "best all-in-one printer"). Each of the examples presents one keyword search or "listener" within your tool. Once you've identified your keyword(s), your social listening tool will search for mentions of these keywords and collect them—in near real time—in an area inside of your tool's dashboard. You'll then be able to take these keywords and pull the data around them into comprehensive reports for your team.

Figure 6-8

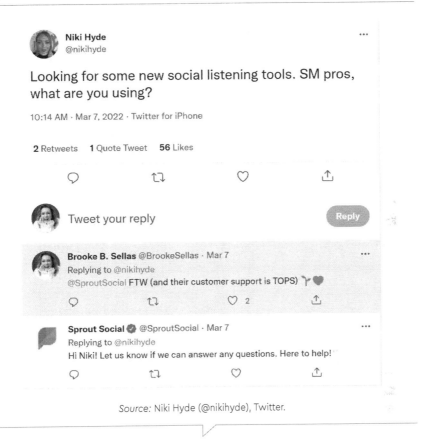

Source: Niki Hyde (@nikihyde), Twitter.

When choosing your keywords, the options are endless. If you're just starting out, I encourage you to focus on the following three main areas. These are very broad verticals but will provide treasure troves of insight:

- **Brand keywords.** Monitoring your company keywords is essential. Examples of our own keywords are our company name ("B Squared Media"), the owner, me ("Brooke Sellas"), our tagline ("Think Conversation, Not Campaign"), and our branded hashtag ("#ThinkConversation"). You can also add keywords like C-suite members and other stakeholders.

- **Industry keywords.** Keywords also can help you glean insight into what's happening in your industry or even find opportunities for conversion. For example, for our industry words, we could use keywords such as "social media marketing" or "social-led customer care." We could also include some synonyms for those words. Finally, we could attach to our keywords phrases like "looking for" or "can anyone recommend" to see the mentions from people online who are looking for services like ours. Now you're not only listening, but you're also finding potential moments to have acquisition conversations.
- **Competitor keywords.** If you've identified your closest competitors, enter their brand or company name as a keyword "listener." From there, look for questions and complaints directed at their brand. These conversations can give an idea of why your brand is doing better or worse—and lead to better messaging for your own campaigns and conversations.

Boolean searches and keywords. Boolean searches can make you a social listening powerhouse, so I encourage you to get familiar with how it works. Boolean searching is built on a method of symbolic logic, allowing you to combine words and phrases using the words "and," "or," and "not." Using these Boolean operators in conjunction with your keywords and keyword phrases will allow you to limit, broaden, or define your search.

Share of voice. In addition to the keywords, you also want to think about share of voice, which is the measure of brand exposure based on social media conversations. When demoing social listening tools, ask if they offer data on social share of voice. It can be measured as a percentage of total mentions within your industry. You can also use it to look at a specific group of competitors. Since a common goal for brands is a better/bigger share of voice, this is a huge area of potential to tap into.

Additional social listening opportunities. If you're not new to social listening, there are narrower verticals that can give you even more insight. Of course, I hope everyone reading this book ends up going into these pockets of information! But I wanted to set them apart as the next level of analysis. Use these narrower areas of data and insights and soon you'll be "cooking with grease" as we say down South. This is where you listen to achieve even greater outcomes.

Use these ideas to extract actionable insights from conversations. I've included both the what and the why of each opportunity:

1. **Audience analysis.** Examine audience preferences (what) to enhance your marketing strategy and inform business and marketing planning (why).
2. **Customer feedback.** Track conversations concerning your brand (what)—whether you're mentioned with a tag or not—to illustrate customer attitudes and gain visibility into customer experience (why).
3. **Consumer research.** Gather insights on vital data such as demographics, including age, gender, geographic location, and device usage (what). Use this information to better understand and reach your customers (why).
4. **Sentiment gauge.** Explore customer feelings and opinions on specific topics, products, competitors, and more (what). Then, you can optimize your position (why) based on the opinions and feelings of your audiences.
5. **Campaign analysis.** Capture audience reactions to marketing campaigns (what) and create succinct reports to measure success of your campaign (why).
6. **Competitor comparison.** Track share of voice, identify industry gaps, and understand consumer attitudes toward competitors (what) to uncover business opportunities (why).
7. **Trend identification.** Track consumer behavior (what) as it relates to your specific topics; stay up to date with trends in your industry (why).

8. **Influencer recognition.** Identify influencers and industry thought leaders based on follower counts or post impact (what) to help cultivate advocates for your brand (why).

Within each of those data sets, you can slice and dice the data points in a million different ways. This will provide you with a stockpile of social media intelligence. Let's look back before we move forward to examples of conversations that connect with opinions and feelings:

- Use social media listening to gather social media intelligence for your brand, industry, and competitors.
- Collect deeper insights via narrower analysis.
- Become adept at listening to conversations about your brand that both @mention you, and don't @mention you, and respond!

I've shown why you must listen and the costs of not listening. You've seen the impact social media listening and social media intelligence can make not only to your marketing, but to your business as a whole. As we end Part I, I want to drive home the point that you must take advantage of the new opportunity to listen to the online conversations taking place around your brand, industry, and competitors. Listening is only the first part. Having conversations that connect is where the rubber meets the road. And that's next.

CHAPTER SEVEN
Having Conversations That Connect

It's easier than ever to build and launch a product (just look at all the mask companies that sprang up overnight when the pandemic began!). But if you want to survive long term, you'll need to set your brand apart. That means you'll need to have clear messaging, superb storytelling about why your product matters (or how it's different) and be willing to converse with your audience along their digital journey. Today's buyers are self-guided: they're making their decisions based on social media and other third-party data not controlled by you, for the most part, so you've got to be able to pivot faster than ever before.

Now that you have your social media intelligence, you should better understand your customers' digital journey (including all the touchpoints). You've identified—and hopefully begun to eliminate—as many potholes as possible. Next, we're going to talk about how to better use social media at these touchpoints—not just make the journey free of bumps, but to engage.

It's time to start having conversations that connect.

Getting Started

First, where do you need to be? Looking at your digital customer journey (DCJ), you should be able to choose your channels based on your audience.

Go where your audience is. You might not be able to reach them on your own social channels, by the way. You'll need to participate as the brand on users' conversations (depending on privacy settings). If there's an organic chance to enter online banter as the brand, join the conversation!

Choose your channels. Be intentional with each social channel you use; don't blast the same content (especially at the same time, for Pete's sake!) across all your channels. You might use Facebook for storytelling and long-form videos, Twitter as your newsroom or place for quick tips, and Instagram as your home for behind-the-scenes team visuals or community polls. Invest in a media mix for each platform.

The social media channels you choose should have meaning to you and your brand. Choose wisely and don't try to be everywhere—or be everything—to everyone. It's been said, but I'll say it again (and again), when building your audiences, no matter the channel, what will be key is making it personal. Choose the channels that will allow you to personalize in a way that lets you connect with your audience.

Timing. Another consideration with conversations happening online is *when* they happen. You want to think not only about what you say, and who you say it to, but *when* you say it. Customer conversations and demand for support (we'll get deeper on support later) happen at different hours of the day depending on the business and the industry. It's wise to monitor and analyze which days, weeks, and months that your conversations see a surge. Reporting by Sprout Social details events around which consumers tend to be active with their social media accounts.[1] The study found that people are most likely to use social media during certain kinds of events, including:

- personal milestones (50 percent),
- sporting events (45 percent),
- natural disasters (42 percent), and
- holidays (42 percent).

However, just because that is when people are most active, not all moments are appropriate for brands to join the conversation. For example, while some 54 percent say they are happy for brands to post during sporting events, brands might refrain from posting during natural disasters, since only 14 percent say they welcome brand posts during that kind of event.[2]

Seasonality. Seasonal trends are a great time to take advantage of having better, deeper conversations. Boost connections with customers by creating educational, entertaining, and inspirational content that sparks conversation around the holidays. Businesses with large volumes of social media conversation should look to beef up their proactive social-led customer care during the holiday shopping season. Be ready with content that answers FAQs and keep lines of communication open between your social media team and the rest of the business.

Surprise and delight: using timing unexpectedly. Hopefully, by now you've identified your brand's digital customer journey, and have multiple touchpoints. But it's important to remember that on social media, you should not "always be closing." If all your touchpoints are transactional in nature, it's time to focus on a little surprise and delight. Connecting with customers outside of the typical touchpoints like birthdays or other personal occasions can really differentiate you from your competitors. One of our team members, Kristy, unexpectedly received a gift with a hand-written thank you note from the team at Chewy, the pet food brand (see fig. 7-1). Here's what she had to say about the experience: "We've been Chewy customers for quite some time. It's not odd to see random boxes from them show up any day of the week. This one was truly unexpected, however. I opened it up and found a card and a wrapped gift. The sweetest card was addressed to me, and the hand painted gift was of our Coco. I suppose they got her picture from Instagram, or her profile on chewy.com. It was hand painted and signed by the artist.

Figure 7-1

Cat mom Kristy sent me a photo of the gift Chewy sent her, and the inspiration, Coco the cat.

Credit: Kristy Morrison.

Truly just such a delightful surprise and for no other reason than they wanted to show us some love."3

I realize this adds even more time and energy to your outreach efforts. But conversing with customers about something other than selling is a smart approach. For a little inspiration, look to some of the crazy non-official holidays that have popped up all over social media. Send your VIPs donuts on National Donut Day or celebrate a local holiday that will resonate with your audience. Growing up in Texas, I can tell you that no one's jewelry box is complete without one (or a dozen) pieces from local craftsman James Avery. So, it makes sense that they celebrated Texas Independence Day (see fig. 7-2).⁴

Choosing timing that resonates with your customers can not only set you apart, but it makes the path much easier for casual, more friendly conversation down the road. Yep—even timing can help you create conversations that connect.

Figure 7-2

Texas-based jewelry brand James Avery has everything y'all need for our oh-so-sacred holiday, Texas Independence Day.

Source: James Avery Artisan Jewelry (@jamesavery), Instagram.

Why making connections can help you beat the algorithms. Before you can have a conversation, you must make connections. Right now, it's harder than ever to continuously connect with your audience on your social media channels because of the algorithms in place. The problem is that much of your content doesn't reach your followers. It takes a lot of time and money to create content, but even once you do all that work, it doesn't mean your content is getting seen by all your followers. In fact, it's not getting to one percent of them. Worse, it's not getting to 0.1% (yes, that's a decimal in front of the one). On average, Facebook engagement rates are 0.09%. That means a Facebook page with about 25,000 followers should expect to get around twenty-three engagements per post on average—twenty-three!

Even back in 2018, Facebook updated the algorithm to prioritize "posts that spark conversations and meaningful interactions."[5] Meaning that Facebook itself emphasized that brands need a lot more authentic connection if they want their content to be considered as an added value in the algorithm.

So, even if you have a healthy number of followers, Facebook's algorithms are keeping your organic content from being seen. And it's not just Facebook—the latest industry research suggests that engagement rates across social media are declining. However, you can be more thoughtful about the types of content that will "survive" those algorithms. How? By using the SPT. The more your content has feelings and opinions, the more engagement your posts will have, which in turn triggers more promotion for your next post. You can beat the algorithm by being more human using opinions and feelings.

Using the SPT for Conversations That Connect

Now that we're about to start having conversations, let's revisit the social penetration theory and those four types of disclosure. As you (now) know, you want to lean toward feelings and opinions in your content. Where possible, you want fewer facts, and almost no clichés.

We need less marketing and more storytelling. Humans connect, bond, and build trust through common experiences and shared emotions. Brands need to start communicating the way humans do. They must participate in conversations using opinions and feelings to build trust and intimacy. That vulnerability is the price of admission. If you enter the space with clichés and facts, you're wasting time and money.

How to participate comes down to listening and contributing smartly, most importantly, by properly using opinions and feelings to connect to your audience. And (sorry, not sorry) most of you are doing it wrong—you're sooo cliché, focusing on content instead of connecting.

Over the next few pages, I'll share examples of brands using opinions and feelings, as well as facts that create good content. What I want is for you to stop doing what most of you are doing, which is cliché content. Think about how these examples relate to you as both a consumer and for your own brand or company.

Clichés

Cliché content is generally the worst option. Ironically, there's a cliché that's fitting here: "do unto others as you would have them do unto you," also known as the Golden Rule. If your brand is only sharing clichés, you'll get the same back. So, keep clichés to a bare minimum. This is part of human psychology. The reciprocity principle is one of the basic laws of social psychology: it says that in many social situations we pay back what we received from others.[6] In other words, if Brooke does you a favor, you're likely to return it to her (woo hoo!).

When it comes to clichés, chasing trends is just another type of cliché content. Clichés are hard to save—they're just almost always doomed to fail in my opinion. That includes jumping on a bandwagon simply because it's trending. For example, the "red flag" trend—this was a Twitter trend where the red flag was used in a social context (used as a warning sign of types of people you shouldn't date). Then brands began adding red flags to their tweets, but it wasn't a disclosure. It was just a way of getting attention but not building intimacy. Many consumers were seen posting tweets about "muting" red flags because it was so overdone. In other words, it became cliché to use a red flag. So, don't be that brand chasing a trend because you quickly just become a cliché.

Facts

Facts aren't as bad as clichés—but they aren't great. Obviously, you should share information that is critical to your community: updates, shipping changes, new store openings, etc. But these are things that don't have emotional value. Most brands are out there trying to persuade their audiences with facts. Remember when the news used to be facts? Now it's more opinion-based or storytelling.

I saw a great example of a truly factual post from the Savannah Bee Company. "Did you know the average worker bee only lives for just five to six weeks?"[7] I did not know that! Most people probably don't know that. Personally, I find this to also be "feelings" content because this made me feel sad for those tireless little bees! There were more than 800 views of the picture of those worker bees—facts can be fun.

Opinions

Opinions don't have to be strong stances on highly controversial political statements. You can invite opinions with things like a poll ("which pen do you like better, and we'll go into production with the one that wins!"). I did a little opinion test myself with the cover of this book! I created three different designs for the book. I had used one version in all my early marketing campaigns because I was sure it was the one everyone would like best. In figure 7-3, you can see

Figure 7-3

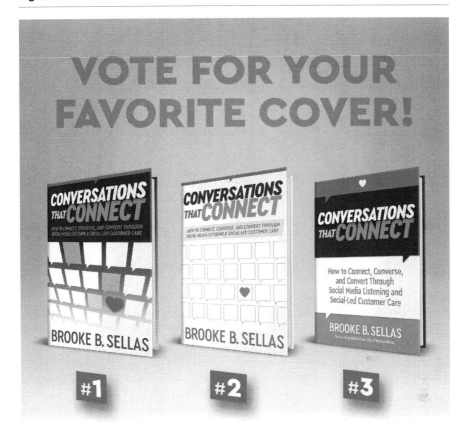

I was so wrong about the cover choice. But your opinion matters more than mine!

Source: B Squared Media.

the three versions that I posted on LinkedIn. I was using version #1. It turned out the majority of people polled liked option #3. And yep—we went with that one—it's the cover of this book.

So, you need to also share your opinion, if you want to get an opinion. You probably post daily to at least four different social media platforms. I encourage you to not only think about sharing opinions and feelings in your online conversations, but creating a good mix of each, using them together for maximum impact.

In figure 7-4, LinkedIn Marketing Solutions is using a poll to elicit opinions (and kinda feelings since they use the word "fun" for business-to-business (B2B) content!).[8] This is such an easy way to get your audiences to converse with you—especially in the beginning or for breadth-type conversations.

In figure 7-5, the AQHA (American Quarter Horse Association) uses a storytelling post to try and attract attention for an article in their magazine.[9] Did it work? I can't say for sure, but with the amount of likes and comments it received (and with the audience sharing their own feelings and stories on the post), I'd say it was a winner. Kids and animals, folks. Always pulling in the numbers!

Feelings

Feelings don't end at "happy" or "sad." Feelings can include an array of emotions used not only to give feelings but to receive them. Think of feeling words as they pertain to the path to purchase: curiosity, anticipation, gratification, confidence, assurance, and likeability. Some brands will choose to connect using feelings about things that are directly related to their brand, some will tie to current events, others will share feelings on critical conversations around social justice or climate change or politics. But what you should see in the

Figure 7-4

Agree or disagree: B2B content can be just as fun as consumer content.

353   40 comments · 10 shares

Source: LinkedIn Marketing Solutions, LinkedIn.

Figure 7-5

Kids and horses, man. People love 'em.

Source: AQHA (@officialaqha), Instagram.

examples that follow, is an alignment of the brand's core values, and their audiences' values.

The following posts are using feelings in the way that I would imagine most brands will—it gets the community engaged, but they are not strong opinions that illuminate their core values—this is more breadth than depth. That's okay. But later we'll look at some examples where brands have decided to share much deeper opinions and feelings. Brands who do this will probably have a stronger relationship with their audience and/or community because they relate to the brand's values (which is harder to compete with), beyond just your products and services.

First, I love how SmartPak, which provides horse supplies and equine supplements, uses both user-generated content (UGC) plus the brand's own copy to demonstrate feelings about their amazing customer service. In figure 7-6, the customer uses "helpful, friendly, and knowledgeable" to describe their customer support.[10] Some of

Figure 7-6

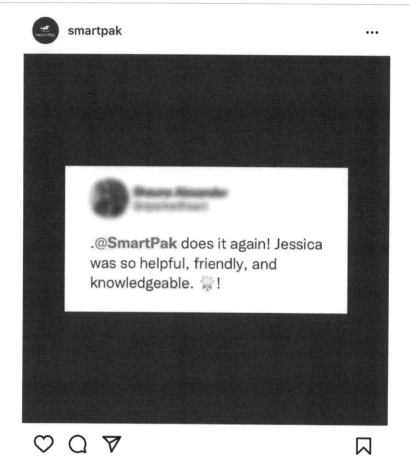

35 likes

smartpak Ever wondered what blanket might fit your horse best? Or how to help support your horse's weight all winter long? Maybe you're wondering how the Hadley breeches fit, or if Piper breeches live up to the hype?

Let our world-class Customer Care Team help! We're all horse people, too, so no question is too big or too small, just give us a call at 1-800-461-8898.

Source: SmartPak (@smartpak), Instagram.

the biggest complaints about customer service—which we'll cover in more depth later—are that customers find support agents to be rude. SmartPak uses customer feedback to let people know they are anything but. This one hits feeling words right on the head in an innovative way—and without the brand trying to "entice" others to give back. The fact that the UGC covers audience/community/customer feelings is just fine.

Walmart has a different conversation with their audience by choosing to go for the intimately personal. For example, they had a "Share Your Dad Story" post in 2021 seeking feelings from their audience in a way that wasn't super obvious. As you can see in figure 7-7, they tried to evoke feelings among their consumer base and online communities.[11] And that can work—if their community thinks of themselves as prioritizing strong family values, they will share opinions and feelings about their fathers. The point is to mirror the values of your audience.

Another example of subdued but effective use of feelings was a post by fast food restaurant, Chick-Fil-A. Their social media posts match their audience by echoing their values, but with less personal reference than Walmart. In figure 7-8, they made a simple post on Instagram celebrating Memorial Day.[12] Presumably they have listened to their audience and know that many of them are patriotic (the post had over 60,000 likes so I think they're right!). As you can see, your "feelings" content doesn't have to be high stakes to get high engagement.

B2B is still B2People. Even if you're a business-to-business company who is selling to other companies, I encourage you to look at all the nuanced ways in which people will buy from you today. Nearly 75 percent of B2B marketers say driving engagement was harder in 2021 than it was just a year before that.[13] Let's face the truth: most B2B content is drab. Essentially, this means B2B marketing needs to incorporate principles of the SPT for more

Figure 7-7

Source: Walmart (@walmart), Instagram.

human-centered and emotionally charged messaging. Assuming you've developed your B2B personas based on your real customers, you should know what emotions to utilize for each touchpoint in your digital customer journey.

Figure 7-9 is a fun post from LinkedIn Marketing Solutions where they share a feeling statement and get feelings and stories returned.[14] (This is a B2B brand! B2B content doesn't need to be dull, y'all.)

My suggested balance of SPT is to make the vast majority of your content opinions and feelings. You can see in figure 7-10 that

Figure 7-8

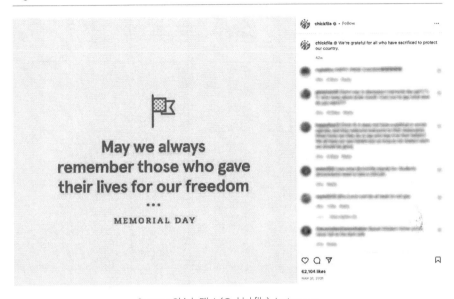

Source: Chick-Fil-A (@chickfila), Instagram.

my recommendation is very different from what I saw in my thesis work—where most of the content stuck to clichés and facts.

Figure 7-9

Source: LinkedIn Marketing Solutions (LinkedIn Marketing), LinkedIn.

Figure 7-10

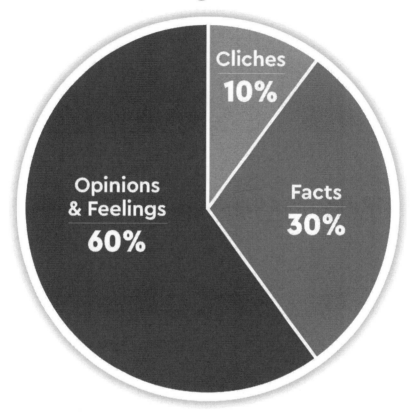

Source: B Squared Media.

Being Right Isn't Risky: Brands That are Fearless about Feelings and Opinions

Look at your audience and the insights you've gleaned from listening to their opinions and feelings: What are their interests, activities, and agendas? Use this as a guide to what *you* should have feelings and opinions about.

If you share opinions and feelings, you are vulnerable. But that vulnerability is what creates connections that lead to relationships. For a brand, those connections create conversations—which are vital to creating communities, to improving customer experience (CX), and ultimately increasing brand loyalty.

When a brand shares a very strong opinion, some potential or current consumers may disagree, even enough to turn away from the product. I get how scary this is. But these are the same choices we make when we build relationships in our personal interactions. Your customers—at least the ones who will ultimately remain loyal—should be aligned with your brand's core values. The better you know your community, the more comfortable you should feel sharing feelings and opinions. However—I cannot overstate this—know your core values, stick to them, and be sure they align with your audience and community. You will be vulnerable. You will lose some customers—we call this "dissolution" in the SPT. You will also build a relationship and loyalty among those who share your feelings and opinions. Let's look at a couple of examples of brands that do this well.

Nike: why they can just do it. A good example of this is Nike's 2018 ad campaign featuring Colin Kaepernick. As I am sure most of you recall, Kaepernick is the NFL quarterback who took a knee when the national anthem played before football games, to raise awareness of police brutality against African Americans and support the Black Lives Matter movement that was working to end it. At that time (and ever since) the country has been divided on this issue. But the entire country is not Nike's audience. It's also worth pointing out that Kaepernick is, of course, an athlete, and they are in the athletic apparel business. And Nike's brand has always supported professional athlete activism and inclusion more broadly. Their decision to choose Kaepernick as the face of a new campaign promoting these values aligns with *most* of the Nike community. But as I said earlier, when you share your opinions and feelings, you will lose those who don't share them.

Much of the news coverage in the days right after the campaign launch focused on negative responses to the ads. (If you don't remember, people posted videos of themselves burning their Nikes in protest of the brand and the ad.) Nike's stock dropped more than three percent the day after the ad campaign was announced. That's a strong response and it makes sense that it grabbed headlines.

But the marketing story, in my opinion, is that a month later, Nike's stock price rose to a historical high, and online sales increased 31 percent.[15] In the first month the ad was on YouTube, it had more than 80 million views.[16] Of course, no one wants to be known as the company whose products are being burned in protest. But Nike had done extensive analysis of their social media intelligence before voicing an opinion.[17] The people who strongly disagreed with their Kaepernick collaboration, burned their shoes. The people who strongly agreed, bought (way) more. Within their community, clearly more people fell in the latter camp. Nike's ad campaign was completely in sync with their core brand values and the values of their customers. Knowing your brand values inside and out, and then aligning those with your core audiences, gives you a much higher payoff than a lower-stake opinion.

Kaepernick took a big risk with his own career by choosing to promote the Black Lives Matter movement. (Kaepernick has not had a contract with the NFL in the years since.) And Nike has long been known for its "Just do it!" slogan which encourages taking big chances. Nike's decision is therefore aligned with a long-held attitude (or feeling).

Ben & Jerry's: bold is their brand. For another example, let's look at Ben & Jerry's ice cream. They've built an empire by taking a stand—they share their feelings and opinions, in no uncertain terms. In figure 7-11, I chose an example of a typical unflinching Ben & Jerry's post.[18]

Figure 7-11

Ben & Jerry's definitely has an opinion.

Source: Ben & Jerry's (@benandjerrys), Instagram.

As you can imagine, not every comment on this post was . . . supportive. But if you are part of the Ben & Jerry's community, I wonder how many were truly surprised. Ben & Jerry's shares opinions on political and social justice issues all the time. They create flavors to support causes (and yes, there was a flavor to support Kaepernick). Ben & Jerry's *is* a political brand. From the very beginning, they have been huge participants in social justice issues, climate change, and other political causes. Their consumers either lean left politically, or don't mind supporting a brand that does. Ben & Jerry's clearly communicates that their political positions are part of their core values. Unlike Nike, they often share opinions on social issues not even related to their industry but are still tied to the brand and culture of Ben & Jerry's. Some customers stopped buying their ice cream when this came out—or at least that's what they threatened in the comments of this post. On the other hand, I would not be surprised if some of their customers shared this post or bought an extra pint or two. But I *would* be surprised if their CMO didn't have a ton of social media listening and analysis in advance that helps them stay aligned with their audience (*and* track the response afterward).

While Ben & Jerry's can safely be labeled a progressive brand, having strong views isn't limited to the left. In 2012, Chick-Fil-A attracted significant negative feedback after sharing their opinions, including their religious beliefs, the decision to be closed on Sundays, and the owners' views on the LGBTQ+ community.[19] They have a longstanding history of donating to charities with practices like conversion therapy, which is hurtful to the LGBTQ+ community. When this was first made public in 2012, there was a lot of public outcry. But they knew their audience, and frankly, it didn't affect their revenue. In fact, sales skyrocketed 12% soon afterward. My point is certainly not to applaud Chick-Fil-A's history. My point is that brands who know their audience know that their core values are aligned. They don't worry about being disliked for their feelings because the dissolution of those who are not aligned is offset by the brand loyalty of those who are. It is worth noting in this case however, that in 2019, after constant backlash against the brand, Chick-Fil-A CEO Tim Tassopoulos publicly announced a change in their giving strategy, though he did not rule out giving to religious groups.[20] (And of course, I will note that not all religious groups endorse conversion therapy or other practices that are hostile to the LGBTQ+ community. I do not know the details of the groups they support at the time of this writing.)

Taking such an unequivocal stance on key issues that impact our society might not only not be that extreme, but it might also be what consumers want. A 2022 survey from Sprout Social reveals the majority of consumers (70 percent) believe it's important for brands to take a public stand on social and political issues.[21] Jay Baer, author of *Hug Your Haters*, supports the Ben & Jerry's approach. In an article he wrote in February 2022, he goes even further—arguing that "broad is flawed."[22] Jay's view is that most brands should be taking a stronger stance—it will ultimately appeal to a narrower, but more engaged audience. He cites research by Accenture that explains how "reimagined customers" want to support brands that share their values. According to the research: "Reimagined Customers see the world through a new lens, and two-thirds of them want the businesses they support to have a similar vision. And not just for products like clothes, or cars. In fact, 44 percent of reimagined customers would change *banks* if their current bank stopped taking sufficient, visible actions for positive social impacts . . ."[23]

It's worth pointing out that Jay personally identifies as a "reimagined customer", so this resonates with him as a consumer as well as a marketer. He advises brands with the following: "Instead of trying to sell to the most people without offense, the new marketing is to sell to people who are aligned with your brand mission, knowing full well that you're going to offend a bunch of others." Many brands are living in "breadth" or "broad" as Jay defines it. They often avoid going into depth (sharing more intimate feelings or opinions) because they fear dissolution. As we discussed earlier, dissolution in the social penetration theory happens when you seek to build deeper relationships with those who align with your brand's core values and you lose those who are not aligned. But I agree with Jay that you also risk not having any deep relationships at all if you don't.

Brand-based risk-taking: Patagonia. Patagonia is another big brand that hangs its hat on taking a stand. They are a little different from Ben & Jerry's because most of their statements are tied to their products. Patagonia frequently talks about climate change. As an outdoors apparel and equipment brand, I would guess that many of their customers are strong believers in climate change. So, while this is an opinion—and a strong one—it might not be that risky for Patagonia. Furthermore, since their product is arguably impacted by climate change, it aligns with the brand. Figure 7-12 is a good example of how they do that.[24] In 2021, they posted a statement on LinkedIn, condemning Facebook for its propensity to spread misinformation about climate change.

You know the phrase "calculated risks"? You can choose to take risks that are less risky in the context of your brand and your audience—particularly your online community. But I suggest you get to

Figure 7-12

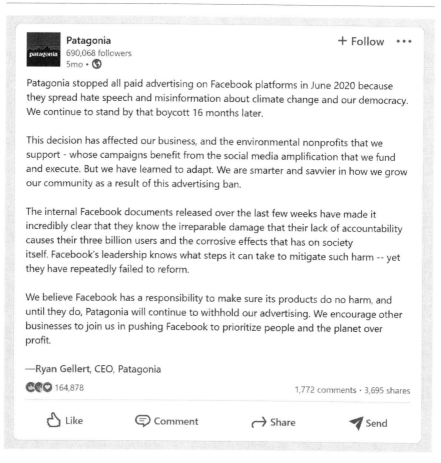

Source: Patagonia (@patagonia), LinkedIn.

know your community with lower risk engagement before you get into the politics and religion space. Just like any other new relationship—get to know the other person before getting into these sensitive subjects.

Going back to the brand Patagonia, they have a good mix of feelings and opinions about the climate which also ties to the brand's consumers. They've also taken a stand about bigger issues and have shared content about Pride and George Floyd, but their mix was far less polarized than the ice cream brand Ben & Jerry's.

So, while taking a stand seems hair-raising, it's just humans wanting to connect with other humans. It exemplifies disclosure levels three (opinions) and four (feelings) of the social penetration theory. Consumers are looking to align and give loyalty to brands who share the same opinions and feelings as they do. We're an extremely polarized nation, and that's no different in business and marketing.

Types of Content: Stories, Questions and (Yes, Even) Sales-Driven Content

Let me be clear: the way to participate in a conversation on social media is not just information pushed out to consumers, which by the way, is still how most brands "market" on social media. It's about participating in conversations to make a connection. Two common ways for brands to start a conversation are stories and questions, so we'll pay special attention to those.

But you're also going to be producing what I call sales-driven content—just being a realist here! However, that doesn't mean it has to be the uninspired content (read: clichés and facts) that I see too often. According to Sprout Social, people who spend time interacting with videos, updates, and blogs are more likely to convert into paying customers.[25] You can sell stuff and inspire—we'll look at some great examples in this chapter.

Stories

I'm using stories broadly in this context. Most of what brands put out as content is a statement or a brief story. It might be something as simple as: "here are our favorite bouquets for Mother's Day." But that's pretty flat, and not likely to get much engagement. Stories that drive a conversation have an opinion, evoke feelings, make you want to reply—even with just a heart emoji. Great stories are rarely driving a sale, or at least, that's not the intention of the story.

A Word About "Stories" as Conversation. I've seen, too often, stories being described by content-focused marketers in a way that is too formulaic and suggests that each step will automatically trigger a response:

1. We are all wired for stories.
2. Tell me a story, and I will relate to you.
3. Once I relate to you, I will like you.
4. Once I like you, I will buy from you.
5. Once I buy from you, I will tell others to buy from you, too (by making you relate to my own story).

That's really an oversimplification. Let me clarify how you create a conversation using "stories." Yes, we are wired for stories. In many cases, to entertain, sometimes to educate, at other times just to relay information. But in this context, we are doing it so that consumers feel as if they can relate to the brand and like it. Which means that your brand's "story" must be full of meaningful disclosures that align with the values of the audience. We don't just hear a great story and say, "I relate to you now! And I like you." When brands share a story, it should contain elements of feelings or opinions, or both.

But the main point is simply that "stories" work in this space is too simplified. A story that doesn't disclose the feelings or opinions of the brand is not a conversation. I would surmise this is one reason marketers spend all that money on content "stories." They think they need these epic stories—when really, they need to share more opinions and feelings. That's what makes a brand relatable or likable.

Ask questions ... and respond

Ask questions—but make sure you're asking questions that elicit opinions and feelings about your industry, brand, or trending topics (that are at least somewhat adjacent to what you do). Keep the conversation going—*respond* to those who give you their time and attention. It not only shows you're listening but makes them more likely to come back time and time again to join your conversations. If you want responses, you must ask for them—you know, the whole "ask and you shall receive" premise. Make it fun, make it light. Eventually you can get to the heavier stuff—remember, breadth and then depth. Start by conditioning your audiences to want to answer you when you come calling. When asking questions on social media pages keep these guidelines in mind:
- Keep it adjacent to your brand or industry.
- Only veer from brand and industry focus if it's trending or seasonal (e.g., holiday-related questions during the holidays).
- Use a call-to-action and specify the outcome or answers you're looking for.
- Don't be scared of open-ended questions.
- Ask questions that make your audience/community the hero.

Bonus points will be given to those who can hit at least three of those in one question! Figure 7-13 is an example from paint brand Sherwin-Williams.[26] They asked their audience what their favorite color is for painting a bathroom—specifically, they asked which color offers a "dramatic splash," to evoke more feelings and opinions. And one of the responses is "super moody and dramatic." The SPT would say this is how we build a conversation—mirroring each other's feelings and language.

You can seed your community with conversational content based on questions highly relevant to them. The trigger might be asking

Figure 7-13

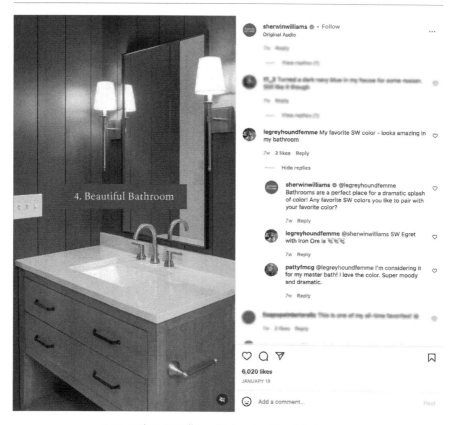

Source: Sherwin-Williams (@sherwinwilliams), Instagram.

(based on your audience) a question they would love to answer; a "lay up" question. For me and other marketers, the question might be: "which social media platform do you hate the most?". I wouldn't be able to refuse answering that one. I love to tell everyone how much I hate Facebook and how awful and morally corrupt they are.

In my Special Olympics example from my thesis work, they asked the question: "what do you think about the 'R-Word'?" Regrettably, for years that word was lobbed at people with intellectual disabilities and is highly offensive. It is a derivative of the outdated medical classification "mental retardation." Asking this type of question prompts their community to respond, and helps the Special Olympics promote inclusive, people-first language, which is part of their mission. In 2010, then-president Barack Obama signed "Rosa's Law," which changed that term to "intellectual disability" in U.S. federal law. The point I'm underscoring here is that these types of questions make you *feel* something. They help the consumer align with the brand.

Another brand that did this well is from my native Texas, where Whataburger is not a fast-food restaurant; it's a religion (just take my word for it). While most brands couldn't start a debate on how to say their name, you can see in figure 7-14 how well it works for them—because they know their audience.[27]

Figure 7-14

WhatAQuestion. And WhatAResponse.

Source: Whataburger (@whataburger), Twitter.

Yep—that's nearly 18,000 likes and almost 1800 replies. And note also that they followed up with another response later in the day. We'll get into replies later, but you can see how they tap into their (very enthusiastic) audience with a question that works for them. And while the question doesn't seem that riveting on the face of it, they knew it would evoke a lot of opinions.

By the way, everyone from Texas knows it's WATERburger.

Sales-Driven Content

Let's talk about the elephant in the room: the content on social media that is designed to promote (sell) your products and services. It's just a reality of doing business, right? But that doesn't mean you can't do so in a way that uses opinions and feelings. I like a couple of formulas that do more than just sell, they frame a problem that the user has and then solves it. These brands hear what consumers want, then offer their solution, in a way that reflects what the consumer asked for. Let's look at some examples:

Problem → Solution → Benefit. In figure 7-15, the makeup brand Blume, shares (very enthusiastic) feedback received after they reinstated the dropper which delivered one of their products.[28] It seems a lot of customers were not happy with the new packaging. I'm sure they learned this from the negative conversation they saw online (social listening). But they heard those statements and brought back the dropper. They then promoted the correction and highlighted the new positive conversation around it (note the opinions and feelings in those customer responses). So, they not only heard the problem—they used it as the basis for promoting the solution. Look at how they took several replies, highlighted them, and answered the outcry of complaints with the Problem → Solution → Benefit formula:

- **Problem.** Repeat the person's problem ("A little birdie told us that a *lot* of you missed the dropper.").

Figure 7-15

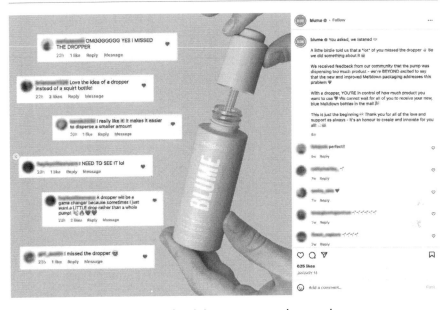

See? Feelings and opinions . . . even about a dropper.

Source: Blume (@Blume), Instagram).

- **Solution.** Present the solution with action steps ("So we did something about it.").
- **Benefit.** Stress the benefit of that solution ("... we're BEYOND excited to say that the new and improved Meltdown packing addresses this problem").

Feature → Advantage → Benefit. In figure 7-16, Cloud Campaign, a social media marketing company, used a post on LinkedIn to go after their competitor Hootsuite with the Feature → Advantage → Benefit formula.[29] The formula goes like this:

- **Feature.** Explain the feature. ("White-labeled dashboard and reports" plus specific features on the itemized list, using bullets that are finger-pointing emoji.)

Figure 7-16

Cloud Campaign
1,416 followers
Promoted

How your agency team will feel after switching to Cloud Campaign Schedule a demo now and get FREE white-labeling on your account (limited time offer).

Explore the social media management platform built from the ground up to help agencies scale. Packed with enterprise features at an entry level price.
👉 White-labeled dashboard and reports
👉 Robust scheduling options for all major social platforms
👉 Effortless content approval process
👉 Agency-friendly pricing with volume discounts
👉 Tons of features designed to cut down on repetitive tasks and save your team time

Schedule a Live 1-on-1 Demo and Say Goodbye to Hootsuite!
cloudcampaign.io

🖊 Sign Up

👍 13   2 comments

Like   Comment   Share   Send

Source: Cloud Campaign, LinkedIn.

- **Advantage.** Present the advantage that feature offers. ("Packed with enterprise features at an entry level price.")
- **Benefit.** State the benefit of that advantage. Notice how they stress the way that this advantage will benefit the customer's scenario, but they do so with *feelings* and *opinions*. ("How your agency will feel after switching to Cloud Campaign," followed by a party emoji, and a picture of real humans with Cloud Campaign swag on throwing a party.)

There are a lot of facts listed here (all their features) but they complement them with images and language that also elicit emotions. By the way, this is a B2B brand—these methods apply to everyone. You can always find a way to include the social penetration theory, and you should!

Replies: Going from Conversation to Community

The way to build a community (which we discussed in Chapter Five: Look Who's Talking—Audience and Community), is to get your audience engaged with conversation. One of the things I want you to understand is that communities are identified and built within the *conversations*; they materialize in the back-and-forth replies, not from content. The initial post you publish is just content. Making an initial post is easy—making an initial post that garners response is less easy—but that's what kicks off a conversation. And as you engage people in the conversation, you begin to understand the areas where you can build a community.

Talking back: best practices for replies. Like everything else social, how to reply is as important as just replying. Saying something is better than nothing ... but let's go for better than nothing. Here are some key points to keep in mind when replying:
- **Care (and quickly).** As in, when someone leaves a nice comment for you, you should take the time to respond. And say more than just thank you—follow up with a question. Try

to entice two-way conversation with your response, when warranted.

- **Hello? Your name is . . . (Personalize.)** By the way, when you reply, use their name! This sounds so obvious and yet I see brands miss this. Responding with someone's name is a big deal, as is signing off with your teams' initials or names. However, research showed that employees only ask for the customer's name 21 percent of the time.[30] I get that is sometimes mitigated with social media profiles showing you a person's name. But for the love of Pete, if someone with the profile name "HelloPrettyKitty" reaches out to you with a request, please ask for their name. People want to connect with people, and getting personal helps set the stage.
- **Offer the assist.** When assisting someone, try taking the conversation beyond your answer to their question and going above and beyond. If it's an acquisition question, you can ask something like: "what can we do to make it to the top of your short list of solutions?" If it's a retention (likely service or support) question, you could say: "what could we do to deliver better service in the future?" Of course, I'd save that one for after a positive transaction has taken place!
- **Be available to explain.** If you're producing how-to content for your social pages, be sure to add that your community managers are there and ready to field any additional questions people may have. Be specific about which channels they're available on and list "office hours" if you've found that many of these questions come in when your team is not.
- **Make recommendations.** If someone is asking about something related to your brand but is not something you offer, don't be afraid to make recommendations of other brands or partners.

The Payoff When You Do Everything Right: User-Generated Content

There can be a big reward when you take the time to think through all the different elements we've discussed, from choosing the right channel, infusing the content with feelings and opinions, and being sure to reply. All of this can lead to an engaged audience that not only is replying, but even begins to produce user-generated content (UGC). When that happens, you can then share (with permission from the user). Ideally, you will benefit from that flywheel we discussed earlier—self-propelling momentum as users generate content that engages more users. This is the holy grail, people! When you're creating your content, be sure to ask for similar stories or experiences from your audiences. This can help you identify UGC.

And you can do this in a sales-driven content context as well. Just look how the brand SnackMagic tackled this in figure 7-17: they used feeling words in their post as well as highlighted UGC (which also used feeling words).[31] Notice they also mirrored the customer's word choice: excitement/excited. They're absolutely selling their product, but it's a lot less in your face with this UGC.

Or, just ask for it. If you've got an engaged audience and ask something too hard to resist, you'll likely still get good responses. A great example of how to get UGC is to just ask for it. In figure 7-18, Ecogold (Not a horse mom? Ecogold makes horseback riding equipment!) just asks for UGC from their followers for a chance to be featured on their blog.[32]

Ideally, your brand will have the kinds of conversations that can build a community generating all kinds of UGC. That's the dream! But realistically, that will take time. And I understand that creating conversations that connect is not easy. It's a lot to navigate. You don't have to do it all at once. But how to prioritize? This is where the DCJ and social listening can be so helpful. If you have spent time

Figure 7-17

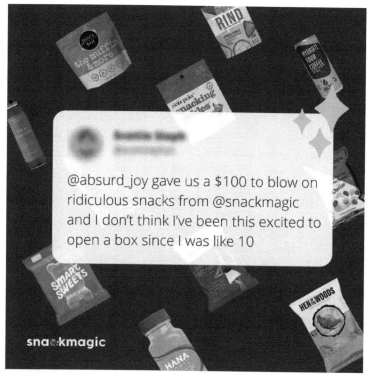

Source: SnackMagic, LinkedIn.

Figure 7-18

Source: Ecogold (@ecogold), Instagram.

really understanding your DCJ, then you know where your potholes are. Produce content that isn't just more cliché noise. Instead, focus on building conversations that meet your audiences where the pain points are. Remember the Blume example? They fixed their packaging and communicated the improvements on social media.

If you have been engaging in social listening, then you also know where you should be. Choose a few key social channels, and produce engaging content of superior quality, and less quantity. Think about which types of content make the most sense for those channels, and for the demographics of your customers. Remember the Chick-Fil-A message about Memorial Day? It got 60,000 likes. The Whataburger poll about how to pronounce their name got 17,000 likes. You should share feelings and opinions, but remember, that doesn't mean they have to be strongly worded stances on high profile issues.

One of the most impactful types of online conversations is social-led customer care. Meeting the needs of your customers and potential customers is key to a satisfying CX. Done correctly, you will not only build connections, but you will also earn loyalty. Social-led customer care is the future—and we're going to talk about that next.

CHAPTER EIGHT
Social-Led Customer Care

The social penetration theory is what will move you from content to conversations that connect. And social-led customer care is what takes those conversations into a fully robust CX that creates true customer loyalty. Social-led customer care goes far beyond customer support (customer service)—this is about a comprehensive approach to your audience and the DCJ. When done well, it can impact almost every element of your operations. And to speak frankly, providing stellar social-led customer and community care means more money. That's right! *Brands with superior customer experience bring in 5.7 times more revenue* than competitors that lag in customer experience.[1]

Great customer care → great CX → brand loyalty. Remember at the beginning, when I said that the pandemic pushed us all online, so now there are almost no barriers to changing brands? The customer experience is what creates brand loyalty. The factors that influence customer loyalty are owned across many departments in your business, but social-led customer care is the hub of understanding those factors.

This is why understanding the correlation between obtaining customer loyalty and how you serve your customers throughout the entire customer journey—including the *digital* customer journey—is critical. Let's take a moment to look at instances that define customer loyalty:

- If you've built a positive relationship with your customer, they're probably "loyal" (until you screw up, that is!).
- Loyalty is tied to a customer's ongoing choice to do business with you.

- Loyal customers refer others to you through word-of-mouth recommendations.
- When you've gained loyalty from a customer, they often give you the benefit of the doubt, meaning you're allowed a small slip up here or there.

Conclusion: Good experiences drive loyalty. Bad experiences drive customers to your competitors.

And social-led customer care is what creates those good experiences. So, let's get into it!

What Is Social-Led Customer Care?

At B Squared Media, we define social-led customer care as learning what your customers value through social media intelligence and then arming yourself with that data to win the war of attention, trust, and loyalty. Social-led customer care is the service of responding to the specific demands, questions, and pain points of your current and would-be customers via social media. A good social media customer care team will engage in ways that leverage your social media intelligence, help you acquire new data, and distribute this information to other departments. What new information should be on the product's packaging, or in the instruction leaflet? What benefits or attributes should the sales team emphasize? Where should the newest brick-and-mortar store be located?

Social-led customer care is the future

Social-led customer care is possibly my favorite part of where we are now with social media. This is one of the places where your company and brand will have the most conversations. Partly this is because it often requires a quick, thrifty response because it does have a significant customer support component.

But customer care, as we discussed in the flywheel, is far more than a call center listening to people's complaints. Yes, that's one part of it. But social-led customer care is far more comprehensive: it should drive how you build your business, develop your corporate culture, deliver your corporate communications, and so much more. It's the same way that early technology was misunderstood—back when information technology (IT) as just the guy who fixed the paper jam in the printer. I love Mark Schaefer's rebuttal for the antiquated "cost center" thinking. This is what he said in a joint webinar we produced on the impact of the pandemic and social-led customer care: "Customer care is looked at the same way we used to view IT in the '90s. It was a cost center. We all wanted to figure out how we could cut costs for the IT department. Now, the IT department is foundational to business; you build upon it, not add it on."[2] Organizations don't just have a technology department to support sales or finance. Now finance and sales departments operate on digital platforms. They're relying on technology to make their decisions.

Customer care will eventually be the same comprehensive driver that IT has become. Customers are the marketer—they tell you if your products are good, if your CX is satisfactory, if your values align with theirs. And brands who understand this will lean into a customer-centric model by making their customer care teams one of their highest priorities. Managing conversations with a brand's community is the beginning and the end of the digital customer journey—remember that the journey is a circle. Brands with fully developed customer care teams will be engaged and meet would-be customers where they first become aware of the brand. And they will engage with loyal customers who they can develop into brand advocates—and help seed conversations for the awareness stage of the next customer.

As much as we would like all our social media conversations to center around acquisition or brand-touting community banter, more and more customers are coming to social media to gain support. Social messaging is the future of customer care. Gone are the days when we pick up the phone and wait minutes or hours for service (while listening to awful hold music, ick!). And email? As I said earlier in this book, social media is poised to take over email in the next couple of years. As the younger generations begin to dominate buying power, more and more of your consumers will expect speed, convenience, and personalization from your brand online (including customer service and engagement on social media). To keep up with digital transformation, it's vital that you start to set benchmarks for how your social media presence is keeping your brand at the frontlines of the loyalty war.

There's also the bottom-line reality of cost savings. Did you know that handling customer support requests via social media channels is up to twelve times cheaper than handling the same requests by phone?[3] Cost savings is just one of the many reasons to consider using social media to converse with customers.

Why customer care supports retention

Think back to the digital customer journey we discussed and the ownership/retention stage. This stage is more important than acquiring new customers when you consider that it's way more cost effective to retain customers than it is to find new ones. Add to that the ever-increasing volumes of branded content being published (and those algorithms, ugh), and it's a given that business owners should be shifting their attention to solving customer issues on social media.

So, if you were to ask me: "where do we start with our digital customer journey?" I'd tell you the retention stage. A company will live or die depending on repeat business. That's true for almost everyone. I don't care if you sell peanuts or planes, there is a finite number of people in the world, so you're going to run out of new customers at some point. Repeat customers are easier to sell to, and usually spend more money over time. They already know you, so it costs less to retain them than new customers who must become aware of your brand, consider you versus your competitors, and then must be converted. Return customers are most likely to be recommenders—or over time could even become advocates. Focusing on retention reduces costs and maximizes profit and makes you more customer centric.

All of this is important in this context, because social-led customer care lends itself well to staying connected with current customers. In the past, you had to send out an email to a list of customers, or advertise to everyone, to reach the subset that was your customers. But now, you can build (or join) your community of customers and engage with them regularly. You can listen to what they say about your products, if their attitude is changing about you, and why. You can find out every day—every hour—exactly what is going well, or not. Loyalty is key to growth, and a good CX is key to loyalty. And knowing everything about their needs and feelings is key to creating a good CX.

Operationalizing Customer Care

As I said previously, social-led customer care shouldn't be confused with traditional customer service. But let's talk about customer support because at a minimum, brands can, and should, be making customer support on social media a huge priority.

Conventional customer support strategies are not designed to meet customer complaints that come through your social media channels. Most often, traditional customer support activities are centralized in its own department. Meanwhile, social-led customer care is often a mix of marketing, social media, and customer support teams. Customer support can be tricky to handle, even with customer support teams at the ready. For one thing, traditional customer support usually means nights and weekends have little, or no coverage. If you use a hotline or send an email after business hours, you probably will not expect an answer right away. But people request customer support through social media at all times and expect an answer quickly.

Another challenge is that the range of support requested through social media will invariably exceed all the information provided to customer support agents. In those cases, the consumer can easily become frustrated as they are handed off to others for help.

From the brand side, and the work we've done at B Squared Media, using social media platforms as a primary contact for customer support (including social selling) is a serious commitment. For one, it's intense and exhausting; social customer care agents must be able to solve a wide range of complex questions as well as navigate customer complaints. In our experience, the biggest missing ingredient to doing this well is organizations' inability to provide round-the-clock staff. In addition, professional providers' social media community managers have a more extensive technical understanding of most of the popular platforms. Since our team deals with several major brands across many industries, it's easier for us to have a "been there, done that" attitude—even with the wildly wacky and woefully rude.

We're going to get into detailed day-to-day processes that we use at B Squared Media. I'll even tell you how we triage issues and build out documentation. But first let's talk about two key areas that should drive how you think about customer care more strategically—creating personalized experiences and acting with empathy.

Personalization

You could say that empathy makes a person feel heard, understand how they are feeling. Personalization helps you feel seen, I know how you feel, *and* I know who you are. Dale Carnegie said: "remember that a person's name is to that person the sweetest and most important sound in any language."[4] But true personalization in social-led customer care goes much further than just knowing someone's name. And when you do it right, it's key to brand loyalty.

The *Next in Personalization 2021 Report* by McKinsey revealed that companies who excel at customer intimacy and personalization generate faster revenue growth than their peers. The closer organizations get to the consumer, the bigger the gains. The brands emerging as leaders in personalization tailor their offerings and outreach to the right individual, at the right moment, with the right experiences. In other words, the superior brands personalize, and as I will explain, the more they personalize, the better they get to know their customers, leading to even more personalization. That is what will keep brand loyalty—you must be the brand that knows your audience inside and out. Here are key highlights from the McKinsey report on personalized interactions:

- **Get personal or get left behind.** According to the study, 71 percent of consumers expect personalized interactions from the brands they use. And, when it doesn't happen, 76 percent of them get frustrated. That's not only bad; it can be catastrophic, because if consumers don't like their experience with your brand, it's easier than ever for them to choose something different. In fact, during the pandemic, three-quarters of consumers switched to a new store, product, or buying method.
- **What is personal, anyway?** Seventy-two percent of study participants said they expect businesses they use to recognize them as individuals and know their interests. When asked to define personalization, consumers associate it with positive experiences where they are made to feel special. That includes touchpoints like checking in post-purchase, sending a how-to video, or asking consumers to write a review.
- **Personalization begets more personalization, which leads to loyalty.** Personalization is especially effective at driving repeat engagement. Even small shifts in improving customer intimacy create competitive advantage—and these benefits

increase over the maturity of the relationship. Those recurring interactions create the ability to personalize even more. The more data they have, and the more skilled they become at applying that data, the easier for brands to design ever-more relevant experiences. This increases customer knowledge and intimacy, generating strong, long-term customer value and loyalty.

As I've mentioned, even B2B buyers expect personalized experiences. After all, there's still a person or group of people on the other side making that buying decision. They too want you to understand what their pain points are and care about solving them. Salesforce highlighted this in a recent study and found that 66 percent of B2B buyers expect vendors to personalize engagement to their specific needs.[5]

Have you started to see a common theme here? The businesses that have customer-centric strategies are outperforming those who don't and using conversations that connect on social media is a surefire way to both acquire and retain customers. In fact, companies that leverage personalization realize 40 percent more revenue growth.[6]

Empathy

When someone reaches out to your brand on social media for customer care, it's a given that they're expecting you to react with empathy. This is an aspect of customer care that many businesses struggle with—handling complaints with massive amounts of empathy. Your team must show up to work covered in Teflon-thick skin, even more so than your typical sales associate in real life. People are willing to be far more aggressive—downright vile, when they can be a "keyboard warrior" and say what they like from the darkness of the internet.

Empathy is not the same as sympathy, by the way. Sympathy is: "aw, so sorry that happened to you!". But the outcome of said thing doesn't affect your day. Whereas empathy is putting yourself in someone's shoes and being affected—and responsible—for the outcome. With social-led customer care, you're likely getting pelted with opinions and feelings (whether you like them or not!). It's important to respond with empathy. We have a formula at B Squared Media for our customer care clients and how to respond with empathy. As you can see in figure 8-1, this formula puts an emphasis on aligning with empathy; you've heard what they're saying and it's valid.

Need more specific responses to help you with empathy? We have dozens that we use, but here's my "top ten" list you get started with the A³ formula when customers complain:

1. I would be frustrated/upset too.
2. [*Doing X thing*] is complicated! Don't worry, I can walk you through it.

Figure 8-1

 Acknowledge + Align + Assurance

1. **Acknowledge:** *Use empathy and acknowledge their issue. Includes acknowledging any frustration.*

2. **Align:** *Align yourself with the community member or customer. Put yourself in their shoes (again, empathy!) and let them know you understand. If it's a big deal to them, it should be a big deal to you.*

3. **Provide Assurance:** *Keep communication lines open if you can't solve their issue with the first interaction.*

Source: B Squared Media.

3. I can imagine how annoying [*insert their pain point here*] would be.
4. That's disappointing. It's especially frustrating when [*insert customer's efforts so far*] don't work.
5. I can see how that made you [*insert/mirror the feeling word they used*].
6. This [*situation*] is unacceptable to us, too.
7. If I were in your shoes, I'd be as [*insert/mirror the feeling word they used*] as you are.
8. As a [*product/service user*] myself, I completely understand where you're coming from!
9. I'll keep you updated. Look for a response by [*time frame*].
10. I see you've been a longtime customer, thank you!

Triage Your Conversations and Build Your Documentation

You can set up social-led customer care or support however you want. Realize also, that potential customers are reaching out to "customer support" and *not* just sales. This is especially true if all your inbound messaging comes in through one main social media handle. In other words, sometimes it's neither customers nor support—it's a potential buyer. Outreach and sales messages meant for potential customers (marketing and advertising) are too often divorced from the problem solving/existing customers ("customer support").

We find the best system is to triage the types of conversations we have so that we can handle them more efficiently. Ideally, you want as much to be in the category of what your frontline team can handle. To do that, we have extensive documentation for each issue. And every time there's a new situation that can't be handled, we update the documentation, that helps us keep improving, become more efficient, and reduce the triage that must leave the main support team.

Build out your "triage" for reactive conversations. Here's how we "triage" at B Squared Media for our clients. We use a stoplight system (green, yellow, red). We rely on extensive documentation so that we can handle as much as possible. Here's how it works:

- **Green.** When it's labeled "green" we can handle it, even as an outsourced partner. That doesn't mean it's "easy," per se, but we have an established protocol. Remember, inbounds can come in 365 days per year, and they can surge unexpectedly. But users will still expect a very timely response. By the way, even if the issues are relatively straightforward, you still need to build connections with your users, responding with feelings and opinions.
- **Yellow.** When we label something as yellow it's usually one of those weird things. This includes questions or requests that haven't come up before. They can probably be turned green after they have been researched. However, some can also turn from yellow to red depending on the situation. We have the term "situational sorry"—and yellows often happen with these. This is when a client doesn't want to say sorry, but we may need to say it, or if not, try to figure out what's going on without apologizing. One thing to note: yellows don't stay yellows—they get resolved to green or transferred to red.
- **Red.** We label things red that must get processed. Perhaps it's something that must get passed to another team (whether outsourced or not). Many times, it's information an outsourced partner or even a frontline customer care team member wouldn't have access to or control over, like a bank balance, or a password. It might require additional steps, such as if a product return is being processed, or a service representative needs to come out and repair a refrigerator. When a request needs to be given to another team this is labeled "red."

In table 8-1, you can see a summary of our stoplight system for customer care triage.

Table 8-1. The Stoplight System: Customer Care Triage

Tier	Types of issues	Team	Tip
Green	Straightforward questions. Simple facts.	Customer care team members.	The better your playbook, the more you can keep in the green category. Bots can be used (sparingly!) for rote information like hours of operation.
Yellow	Weird questions. Outside the playbook. Complicated issues.	Triage. Transfer to another team or escalate to senior care team leader.	Over time, you should keep updating your documentation so you can move some yellow issues to green.
Red	Secure issues (customer banking details). Issues requiring follow up (in-person repair).	Triage	Some brands may find it helpful to embed a member of the relevant team with customer care for faster resolution.

Source: B Squared Media.

Documentation

As you can see, we aim to handle as much as possible. But when we can't, we try to learn from the situation and update our documentation so that the next time we can take care of it directly.

Set up an internal customer support FAQ document. This should be a living, breathing document which takes all the questions you have ever gotten, and puts those questions—and answers—into a shareable document. It must be shareable so that every team member or person (not robot) helping with these conversations can use it to answer questions according to your brand guidelines. And it really is a living, breathing document because your internal team will always get new and wonderfully weird questions from customers/users/trolls. Hey, people are strange (as *The Doors* said), and give you their weirdness like it's a gift, so you must continuously iterate and pivot. (Does anyone else internally scream, "Pivot!" like Ross Gellar on *Friends* when they see the word? No? Just me? Cool...)

The FAQ document and the triage process feed each other: the more situations you have tracked in the document, the fewer "yellows" you must label because you have a proven procedure for moving them to green or red. And the more situations that go through triage, the more you keep updating the FAQ. All of this helps you become more efficient, which saves on human hours, resulting in real cost savings.

Create a rules of engagement document. How and when you engage with certain users on certain platforms will differ based on your own company's social media goals, social media policies, and other aspects of how you do social media marketing and support at your organization. This document should outline responsible engagement by those who will be performing those tasks. Emphasize the behaviors your team can and cannot engage in while on social media. For example, you could tell them to refrain from joining sensitive topics, such as politics or religion, or avoid attacking competing companies. Remind your social team how they're expected to use social media to communicate and connect with others to build relationships and value. Tone and voice guidelines should be included here. Does your brand use exclamation points? Emoji? Gifs and memes?

Additional documentation. Here are some additional situations that will need documented guidelines. Note that these situations can be difficult to figure out and appropriate guidelines may require time to develop:

- how to deal with irate customers who won't move to private messages or DMs,
- how to deal with trolls,
- when to delete comments,
- when to block someone, and
- how to handle influencer or partner inquiries.

There are also nuanced circumstances that only some of you will face. Some instances of "what to do next" are very situational. During those events, we found it helpful to create "if/then" documentation. In other words, *if* you see a certain type of content (like your reseller posts something, which shouldn't be tagged the same as your audience tagging *then* you document differently (have a set of tags for reseller posts).

No matter the size of your business, you need to have documentation. It doesn't have to be complicated, either. At the very least, I'd have the following written out clearly for your social media marketing and support teams:

- social media marketing policy,
- team hierarchy (with list of people in each role),
- social media marketing plans, including your content and service strategy,
- social-led customer care documentation,
- usage/monitoring/engagement policies, and
- privacy and permissions documentation.

If needed, collaborate closely with your compliance team to understand—and abide by the latest regulatory compliance policies your company needs to follow. And make sure they're included when you make changes!

Accounting for the conversations you'll be tracking (we'll discuss this more in Chapter Ten: Coding Conversations) and the support documentation you'll need will not only help you run your business, it will make information sharing among your teams more efficient. Really well-organized documentation also means that you can likely cut human costs since people can access information quickly and use it again when needed (and all on their own). In any case, effective marketing documentation will help bolster your conversational content strategy, and it will help the teams who manage them have autonomy and efficiency—which we'll jump into in Chapter Twelve: Teams, Not Tech.

Embrace the Negative Nancys

When I say embrace Negative Nancys, I don't mean you have to love the customers who have a negative attitude. What I do mean is focus on the negative feedback you come across, especially where there are "clusters" of such complaints. One of the most effective ways to reduce the cost of serving customers—whether it's in real life or digitally—is to eliminate the root cause of frequent pain points. And social-led customer care is particularly well designed to find how often people are complaining about certain things. We'll dive into tagging and sentiment later, but for now, suffice it to say that it is much easier to analyze social media intelligence using social-led customer care than, for example, analyzing call center data.

Our client, BCU, provides this example of focusing on the negative. In the credit union world, intermittent system downtime—especially if unexpected—may impair users' ability to move money, perform transactions, and make payments during the affected time. Downtimes can happen when financial institutions are working to scale their payment infrastructure to support the rapid growth of digital banking adoption. Think of it as a software update: part of what our client wanted to understand was what were the major customer complaints during scheduled system maintenance periods, despite their best efforts to schedule the downtime during the overnight hours.

Using social listening and sentiment scoring (more on both later), we were able to track and label all the negative chatter that happened during one of their scheduled downtimes. What we found was that 80 percent of customer complaints were about the fact that overdraft protection was not available or active during the downtime (see fig. 8-2).

Since this wasn't mentioned in the downtime notice, customers felt caught off guard. As I mentioned in Chapter One: "Where Do We Start?" when discussing consumerism in crisis, transparency is not

Figure 8-2

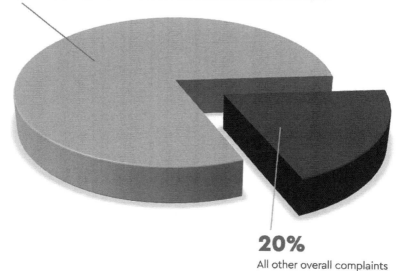

80%
Complaints about the bank's lack of transparency, the declined credit cards and the unavailability of overdraft services that had not been disclosed

20%
All other overall complaints

Source: B Squared Media.

only critical for consumers; it's expected. Quantifying this data for the top executives at the credit union solves two things: (1) we were able to answer the question of *why* ("why are our customers so unhappy with downtime?"), and (2) we were able to show that 80 percent of the why was something that could be fixed. For future downtimes, simply alerting the customers who most frequently took advantage of overdraft protection that this feature would not be available during planned maintenance might be enough to prevent customer dissatisfaction. But BCU took it further than that. They decided, based on this research, to extend the grace period during downtimes to ensure their customers could avoid needing overdraft protection anytime the system was unavailable for scheduled maintenance.

And then they went even further. As a result of the listening, they increased the overdraft protection—not just for downtime periods, but for *all* periods. Being proactive is everything and goes a long way to endear your customers to your brand. Remember what Jay Baer said about reimagined customers willing to switch banks? This example from BCU is one of the many ways a brand can stay innovative with digital transformation.

Part of being proactive means using the social media intelligence you're gathering from conversations—good or bad—and passing those insights to a team or department who can address the source of the issue. If you aren't being proactive, you aren't using your resources effectively. *This* is what leads to customer support being a cost issue. Being reactive in today's climate is a surefire way to fail.

Bad customer service is expensive. Would you like to know what costs you (a lot)? Bad customer service. Social media has empowered people to share the truth about their experiences with businesses and brands (and thousands of onlookers!). So, you can thank the internet for increased visibility and sales, and that your customer complaints now come in the form of rage tweets, Facebook rants, and awful online reviews. Taking to social media to spread woeful tales of terrible service to the masses has almost become an artform for some. This costs you because after more than one bad experience, about 80 percent of consumers say they would rather do business with a competitor.[7] Even better, permanently remove the pothole to avoid future bad experiences, which is cost effective (time saved from future customer support conversations). Let's look at an example of a client that did that.

The cashback app bug. Another one of our financial clients has a cash back app. We discovered via social media intelligence that several customers were running into the same issue: they were not seeing their cash back show up after purchasing from one specific partner, a grocery store. The B Squared Media team could have responded to each person, giving them the workaround to see the cash back points that were missing, and get positive feelings returned each time. However, by repairing the pothole itself instead of continuing to drive around it removes the issue for everyone. Many times, your goal is simply to solve the problem, and that will turn a frustrated consumer into a happy one.

In this case, our client was able to remove the problem altogether. Their developer removed the bug that was causing this glitch instead of our team answering the same questions over and over. That's more cost efficient than agents going through the steps with each person. Finally, an upside of social media customer care is that you can also easily announce these updates. Tweet the update out to your community, which you can't do in traditional customer support environments like a call center.

One more thing about Negative Nancys and how they can help. Remember that Blume brand that got negative feedback about the dropper on their bottle? When they reinstated the dropper, they announced it on social media. Social-led customer care gives you an opportunity to resolve negative situations one-to-one, while using social media to leverage the one-to-many. Here are a couple more customer care opportunities:

- **Reviews.** Ask for reviews (from enthusiastic customers) on your social channel of choice. Ninety-four percent of consumers say an online review has convinced them to avoid a business.[8] So, the more positive reviews you can get from happy customers, the better. Don't forget to respond to reviews—including the not-so-stellar ones.
- **Product updates.** Post about product updates, especially if it's something compelling. Give your customers, community, and audience a sneak peek of what's coming. It will make them feel special and can build stronger connections as well as show the value of following your brand on social media.

Customer Care Is Not a Cost Center! But No Care Will Cost You

As you can see from the examples, customer support (and customer care more broadly) is not easy. But I hope you also now see how it can be vastly impactful on your business, across multiple departments. Supporting your customers on social media should not be viewed as a cost center. It is central to customer experience and done properly should be informing your sales strategy. Too many businesses and brands aren't investing resources into digital customer care channels because they view it as a cost. If your current social care goal is making customers happy while "doing more with less"—you're doing it wrong. Customer relationships are the key to today's online marketing landscape, while poor customer experience can damage the reputation of your brand in an instant.

Once customers are disappointed, only 18 percent will keep their business with that brand, and only 15 percent will recommend the brand to friends and family.[9] Let me phrase that the opposite way—you could lose more than 80 percent of your customers if you don't meet their expectations. Does investment in their happiness sound like a cost center in that context—or the lifeblood of your business? The path to uplevel your digital customer experiences isn't a massive investment in digital transformation. It's a mindset along with a series of small changes that add up to a significantly better customer experience. Remember what I said about CX and potholes in Chapter Three: The Digital Customer Journey? It's not about rolling out the red carpet, it's about reducing clicks, or pain points, or time to resolution.

Social-led customer care is a hugely untapped opportunity. But we have a long way to go in doing it well. A national survey stated that 75 percent of consumers reported worse customer service experiences since the pandemic started.[10] According to the study, the top reasons for customer irritation included not being able to speak to a real person, long wait times, agents taking too long to resolve issues, agents not having a solution or advice, and agents using scripts instead of organic interactions. With all this, you can see why complaining is on the rise. But people are not just complaining to the brand—they are complaining to other people (current and potential customers).

According to *The Wall Street Journal*, overall customer dissatisfaction has increased. In 2017, 56 percent of consumers said they experienced a problem with a product or service. By 2020, 66 percent of consumers were dissatisfied.[11] And that's a real problem because as you can see in figure 8-3 dissatisfied consumers tell twice as many people about their experience as satisfied customers.[12]

However, studies show that when complaints are handled to a customer's satisfaction, they become more loyal than before they had the problem. Think about that for a minute because that's huge.

Figure 8-3

Satisfied customers tell 3.7 people about their positive experience.

Unhappy customers complain to 7 people!

Source: B Squared Media based on data from *The Wall Street Journal*.

You can turn a disgruntled customer into a loyalist through effective customer support conversation (and eventual resolution of that problem). Conversations that connect will help you win the war on loyalty. And revenue. If you come away with one thing from this book, I hope it's this: A complaint isn't necessarily just a negative event. With the right customer care strategy, it can become a relationship-building event. Which is why my answer to "where do we start?" is with the negative complaints and potholes that exist in your customers' digital journey. Yes, it's hard to get it right. But it's often easy to fix what's wrong.

Just look at the top reasons people say a brand's customer service is lacking. As you can see in figure 8-4, the top three are pretty simple: (1) don't be rude, (2) make people feel valued, and (3) have the necessary knowledge or expertise to be helpful.[13]

These should be made a top priority for your social-led customer care team and support agents. Social customer care can't solve these

Figure 8-4

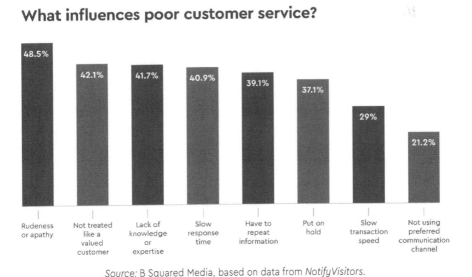

Source: B Squared Media, based on data from *NotifyVisitors*.

issues in and of itself, you still must be present, be human, and be timely. But it does lend itself to addressing some of these problems because you can respond quickly, you can do it with empathy, and you can build a playbook to help you give helpful information.

To do those three things well, you must assist your customers with empathy and understanding at their moment of need, without making them wait. If your customer was at your brick-and-mortar store, you wouldn't dare ignore someone who asked for assistance. But being ignored is woefully common outside of in-person communication. One study found that customers get a response on social platforms only about 50 percent of the time.[14] That's not a slow response—that's no response at all.

If you're not responding to these customers, you are (1) not making your customers feel valued (rude!), and (2) missing out on conversations that connect and that could influence loyalty and retention. The way you support online inquiries and interact with your customers shows how much your business is to be trusted. Answering all direct social media mentions sends a clear message. This demonstrates that you are not only actively watching (and hopefully listening) to what's happening online, you're also an active participant. According to *Hug Your Haters*, "failing to respond on social media can trigger a 43 percent decrease in customer advocacy; a reply, however, can give you a 20 percent bump."[15] Simply stated, social-led customer care is a springboard for new customer acquisition, brand loyalty, and advocacy.

Take Tech Seriously

Part of what overwhelms clients who come to us for help is the constant barrage of mentions—this is especially true for enterprise-sized brands or brands with high volumes of conversations happening through social media. We're talking about thousands of mentions in the span of one hour. Filtering through each of those without the

help of tech would take massive amounts of time (and is probably one reason why the C-suite still looks at social support as a cost center). We utilize Sprout Social's Smart Inbox,[16] which helps us unify our social channels into a single stream to monitor incoming messages, foster conversations, and respond to our audience quickly. It also has "inbox views" to allow our teams to customize their inbox in Sprout to focus on the messages that are most relevant. With a feature like "inbox views" you can:
- optimize your workflow by saving the filter sets you frequently use,
- prioritize among your team by collaborating with specific team members to create and share focused inboxes, and
- manage your workflow from a comprehensive single-stream view without scrolling across multiple columns.

There are many other tools that do this for social media marketing, and many that do this specific to digital customer support. I encourage you to test many of them as you make your decision. Make the salesperson show you (not just tell you) how something works. Explain your goals for using their product. During the demo, ask them to show you exactly how to accomplish what you need. I won't name names, but even some of the bigger tools have a terrible user interface. This makes things messy and inefficient. Choosing the right tool is crucial to thrive. Check out the Resources section at the end of this book for more tool recommendations.

Finally, while self-service tactics like artificial intelligence (AI) and bots are growing rapidly, nearly every digital touchpoint still needs knowledgeable humans. I will keep pulling out my soap box to reiterate that. In fact, I'm going to step up now and talk about that in the next chapter—how we use technology and humans together. They each have their limitations but used together can be incredibly efficient for a greater customer experience.

CHAPTER NINE
A Word on Automation and Bots

I feel like we need a quick sidebar about automation and bots. As much as we are now living in a digital, technology-driven world, reliance on tech in terms of communication (bots, for example) is one of the areas where we should discuss the risks. Many marketers assume that chatbots can be a more cost-effective way to manage social-led customer care. Indeed, chatbots can be wonderful additions to some customer care and community management efforts. From the consumer side, they can (1) answer FAQs twenty-four seven with 100 percent accuracy, (2) provide communications instantaneously to multiple users at once, and (3) multitask, including logging data in real time. On the brand side, bots can both reduce the costs of human capital and team fatigue.

Research from leading chatbot company ubisend explains why consumers are willing to work with bots. You can see in figure 9-1 that humans aren't necessarily clamoring to talk to robots because we prefer them to humans.[1]

Only 19 percent of those surveyed said that human interaction *isn't* important to them. What's more telling is the top reason people turn to bots: they want an instantaneous answer.[2] This tells me that people associate bots with being able to get an answer quickly. So, what brands ought to focus on is response time. Where a bot can give a helpful answer quickly, then a bot could be the perfect solution. It also means that when people are needed, they must also answer a question quickly—this is key, and we'll talk about it more later.

Figure 9-1

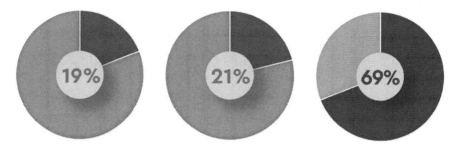

Source: ubisend, "2022 Chatbot Statistics—All the Data You Need."

AI and Customer Support

Artificial intelligence isn't the only way—or even the right way—to solve all customer support challenges. But it can be a great solution for certain needs. These days, most brands offer a variety of customer support channels: call centers, AI-powered chatbots, messaging apps, and even self-service knowledge hubs. And when you do it right, AI can be a fantastic solution.

Nestlé's Ruth hits the sweet spot with AI. Nestlé's bot Ruth is a perfect example because it answers straightforward questions about baking. The bot can manage a lot of data (tons of recipes), but there are no judgment calls to make. And I'd guess most people aren't having huge cookie emergencies, so the stakes are relatively low.

Food and beverage brand Nestlé had more and more customers calling their helpline asking for troubleshooting tips regarding their original Toll House chocolate chip cookie recipe. Their customer support agents ranged in levels of baking expertise, which led to highly inconsistent customer experiences. Nestlé's solution was Ruth, an AI-based digital human. She is named after Ruth Wakefield, who invented the Toll House cookie.[3] Launched in February 2021, Ruth helps Nestlé customers bake and customize their cookies. As you can see in figure 9-2, Nestlé has positioned Ruth as a baking expert capable of providing personalized experiences for people based on their dietary preferences and language, improving CX.[4] Isn't that sweet?! (Sorry, couldn't resist.)

When bots go bad. But problems can arise when brands begin relying on bots for things they don't do well. For example, chatbots rarely convey empathy. Therefore, they may not be a great choice for service-oriented businesses that require sensitivity right from the first interaction. Therefore, if you handle people's money or health or even their internet access, you're probably dealing with customers

Figure 9-2

No, she's never baked a thing. Ruth is Nestlé's baking bot.

Source: Nestlé company website.

who are particularly stressed when there are problems. It's difficult to create appropriately empathetic responses via a bot when someone's credit card isn't working, or their prescription isn't covered by their insurance.

Chatbots are more useful for frequently asked questions (FAQ)—such as what your business hours are or what sizes your products come in. Customers with complex or high-stakes questions (is my doctor in-network?) will probably prefer to speak with a human. They're looking for empathy, understanding, and personalization. Chatbots also make less sense for your business if you do not get the same questions over and over. For example, I can imagine law firms and accountants getting such specific questions that chatbots would struggle to give a helpful response.

AI: If You're Artificial, You're Not Accountable

At B Squared Media, we always remind clients that it's about "teams, not tech." When it comes to conversations that connect, humans must take the lead. The importance of people versus tech is twofold. First, there are the pragmatic limitations of technology to synthesize and iterate actual consumer needs. This continues to improve but humans are still needed to make nuanced, sophisticated decisions. Second, bots can't empathize and connect on a deeper level. This means the investment in humans at certain touchpoints along the digital journey can critically impact relationship building that leads to acquisition, retention, and advocacy.

Therefore, I want you to conscientiously consider a robust investment in people. At certain points in the digital customer journey, they can give a much bigger return on investment because of those two capabilities. It's natural to think of investment in technology as more efficient or providing you with cost savings. But it's not more efficient if you're using tech and automation in ways that don't recognize its limitations. If it's unable to answer the kinds of questions your customers are asking, you're wasting money on tech and creating inefficiencies (a human still must get involved to help the customer, who likely is now angrier than ever).

Earlier, we defined social media intelligence in part as *"collective tools and solutions."* While the tech, artificial intelligence, or bots often scrape and collect data, it's the humans that design detailed and creative solutions from that data. You really need both. Automation is great, but at B Squared Media, we've seen firsthand that combining technology with actual humans enhances customer relationships. AI can never be held accountable; therefore, AI must never drive a management (or creative) decision. I love this quote from E.O. Wilson which sums up how "synthesizers" will live with the constant influx of technology: "We are drowning in information, while starving for wisdom. The world henceforth will be run by synthesizers, people able to put together the right information at the right time, think critically about it, and make important choices wisely."[5]

The coffee crisis. At one time, our client, a luxury appliance brand, had a large amount of negative sentiment around a new product launch. Our social listening tool is what initially alerted us to this fact with auto generated data sets and sentiment scores (more on those later) around the new product's keywords. That was the right role for the technology—to identify and synthesize the data, to tell us what and where the pothole was. However, once we found these insights, it was our job to dig in, discover *why* the pothole existed, and to come up with a solution for the client to smooth out the road.

When we looked at the word cloud surrounding the negative conversation, we found the word "coffee filter" mentioned over and over. And when we dug into that, we saw through the conversations taking place that people couldn't figure out how to change the coffee filter (in their very new, very expensive machine). The tools did all the heavy lifting for us to this point, but none of that includes the solution! We asked the company where the customer could find out how to change the coffee filter, and learned it only existed in a very long product manual. But no one wants to look for page 453 in a user manual to change a coffee filter—especially when it's a luxury brand.

So, what did we suggest? Creating a video, showing people—versus telling people—how to change the coffee filter. That solved several things. First, the video came in handy when customer support agents were replying to negative conversations as the brand. But also, the first thing people do when they have a problem like the one we're describing is Google it ... and guess what shows up in the first few results when this particular problem is searched? The video! People love instantaneous answers, remember? That was the story of the bots. And being able to Google the problem and get led right to an answer (provided by the brand), is another way to give people what they really want—fast response times.

Our social listening tool, while crucial in bringing the data to our attention, could not create the video solution. That took human brain power. Most creative decisions can't be solved with tools or bots. Remember that as you embark on your own journey of collecting social media intelligence.

People, Not Machines, Manage Knowledge

Another reason we say "teams, not tech" at B Squared Media is that machines do not manage knowledge. What do I mean by managing knowledge? Just as I've shown in several of our case study examples, it's our team who manages the creative solutions, or knowledge, not our tools. Your tools will be pivotal, yes. But they are there mostly to provide you with the ability to manage your files, which form knowledge, and the automation to manage those files more efficiently. Here's a useful definition for what it means to manage knowledge: "Knowledge management is the implementation of systems and processes that actively expand codified knowledge, enrich, and organize it for locatability, structure it for use in all channels, and maintain the full lifecycle including actively destroying assets which are ROT (redundant, obsolete, trivial)."[6]

Tools are only as beneficial as the users who manage them. If inputs are poor, insights will be as well. Garbage in, garbage out, as we say. A machine cannot be held accountable. Therefore, your machines shouldn't be making decisions that need accountability.

Managing knowledge, and subsequently knowledge transfers, is one of the key components of a strong customer experience. Realizing the value of humans over machines in this regard can lead to significant advantages over your competitors as we hurtle toward digital transformation.

CHAPTER TEN
Coding Conversations

Now that we have all our social listening happening, and we're engaging in the right conversations, with the right people, in the right places, we need the machines. Remember, the machines are helping us gather, tag, label, and score our conversations for sentiment. They're not connecting with feelings in conversations and helping us support customers with empathy. To do that, you'll need humans to use the data you're collecting with social media intelligence.

The biggest goal of coding conversations is to figure out how to connect with your community using opinions and feelings. This is one of the payoffs of all that observing and listening you did in Part I—you know who your audience and community members are. Now you want to use that data to help mirror their feelings and opinions, their words, their values, their interests.

For us, best practices behind conversations that connect start with the tactics on the backend, before the public-facing strategy. But in theory the pragmatic backend and frontend tactics are happening simultaneously. I will address what's happening both behind-the-scenes and in real time as conversations are coming through on social media channels or through social listening efforts.

Let's assume you have a badass social media tool. (If you don't, you'll see that I listed a few I know to be good in the Resources section at the end of this book.) Over the next few pages, I'll outline the behind-the-scenes work that goes into collecting data with that tool to have better conversations. And you know, to quantify all of this "woo woo" speak to the C-suite.

Tagging

Let's start with tagging. Some social media tools refer to tagging as labeling. You'll want to tag or label both outgoing and incoming conversations. The outgoing conversations are yours—the brand. And the incoming conversations are the conversations from your audience, community, and/or customers.

Creating your own tags

When creating your own tags, you should think first about what you want to achieve, and then you tag to get the information that you need. *Tagging metrics* help you analyze the questions and the topics your would-be and current customers are most frequently asking. *Tagging reports* allow you to assess the tag activity, volume, reach, and performance patterns on both your content marketing efforts as well as any conversation or social-led customer support activities.

Acquisition and retention tags. One of the easiest and first set of tags I'd set up is "acquisition" and "retention." Then, start tagging your incoming inquiries with "acquisition" or "retention" so you can start to quantify the breakdown of these asks from potential customers and actual customers. I have a sneaking suspicion the C-suite will start to pay more attention to social-led customer care as soon as they see that sales opportunities are part of it, too.

One way to quantify this for your C-suite is to tag or label—with your social listening tool—all the incoming conversations to the brand as "acquisition" or "retention." Is it a pre-purchase question or a support question? I ask this because most of our clients assume that the chatter will be almost entirely around existing customers (retention inbound questions). But—they were wrong. And honestly, I think happy to be wrong because they soon discovered a lot of conversion opportunities—not just retention scenarios—were occurring.

We asked each of our social-led customer care clients what percentage of the social chatter around their brand was pre-purchase or post-purchase. Their answers ranged somewhere from zero to five percent pre-purchase. Meaning, they believed that pre-purchase or social selling conversations (awareness and consideration stages) were all but nonexistent.

However, as we started instituting this practice of tagging all incoming conversations with "acquisition" or "retention" we found that there was a huge number of acquisition conversations. In fact, with our technology client, we soon discovered that we were tagging more than 20 percent of social chatter as acquisition—meaning people asking questions in the buying moment! Two of their product lines had 60 to 70 percent of the conversations tagged as "acquisition"! Over the course of just a month, we had dozens of acquisition-inbounds per product line. We started testing this more broadly, and for nearly everyone, "acquisition" tags were at least five percent, but as you just read, it was sometimes well over that.

Now armed with that information, we knew the client should spend more time on social-led customer care regarding acquisition and conversion conversations. In fact, the technology client ran to their sales team with our social media intelligence to have them create more nurture content around the frequently asked pre-purchase questions that were coming in via social media.

As my friend and colleague Linleigh Marie Kraft, who is senior manager of social at a global technology company, said:

> That's really the beauty of "social" media, isn't it? The power to open the lines of communication between your brand and its consumers— no matter where they are on their customer journey. That said, the added knowledge of where they are is important to enhancing their brand experience and your overall brand perception. Therefore, there's more to acquisition and retention tags than quantifying online conversation. If done right, they should help you to activate at scale—providing you with invaluable insights to enhance everything from your customer experience to content strategy, product

development, and more. These tags make you the voice of the consumer and act as signals and directives to your teams.

Linleigh went on to explain how these tags offer multiple advantages:

> For example, they help your community management or customer care teams direct customers more effectively—resulting in better overall customer experiences and an opportunity to authentically recommend products. They help you discover and fill content gaps that allow you to align your content strategies with the needs of your consumers. They help your product teams better analyze and action product feedback. And the one we all love, they help you garner buy-in from leadership by showcasing the value of organic social. All-in-all, knowledge is power—for both you and your customers—but it is what you do with it, how and when you show up for them, that enables you to learn and grow together.[1]

What if you gave your social-led customer care teams a "house tab" the way bars do for their bartenders? (It always goes back to beer!) Bartenders are often given a "house tab" each night to comp drinks and generally make the experience better. They can use it as a "just because" or maybe there was a long wait for a drink and the tab was used as a way to say sorry. What if social support teams had this same kind of "house tab"—maybe a small budget to offer a giveaway during pre-purchase, for example? If they could financially incentivize some of those customers who are in the buying moment don't you think they could sometimes close the deal, then and there? My money's on yes.

Naming tags by product line. If your brand is product led, you'll also want to create a tag for each product. For example, with our luxury appliance brand, we may tag incoming conversations as, "refrigerator_[*product name*]," "icemaker_[*product name*]," etc. With tagging, we learn which products and services have the most conversations. We can also see when these conversations happen over time, helping with seasonal trends and timelines.

For brands with numerous product lines, tagging is critical. You can tag each product line as well as each individual product to get a handle on (1) how much content is going out from you (the brand) on each product, and (2) how much conversation is generated by your audiences about each product/product line.

Other tags. We also tag for things like "feedback" or "review," meaning if someone leaves feedback (good or bad) about a product or service during the conversation, we want to note that. Feedback isn't an official review but it's just as important. If something feels like a review but hasn't officially been entered as one by the person giving that stellar write-up, we tag it as such. Then we ask if they'd be willing to copy and paste it on an official review site, like Google My Business or Facebook. Obviously, those public reviews are gold for brands!

Sentiment Analysis

We tag the sentiment of conversations (negative or positive) as well. Sentiment—the feelings that potential or current customers have about their interactions with your brand—is hugely important to differentiation. Marketing and sales departments often know what happened, but they have a harder time answering *why* it happened—this is what sentiment analysis provides.

- Why do customers buy from us?
- Why do potential customers buy from our competitors?
- Why is product or service X under or overperforming?

Knowing the answers to questions like the above are imperative to a business and this is where sentiment plays an important role. I want you to think of sentiment analysis as a subset of social listening. While you should (obviously) monitor your brand mentions, sentiment analysis goes a layer deeper to understand the positive, negative, and neutral emotions adjacent to those mentions.

As I've stated earlier, you can get sentiment scores as an out-of-the-box functionality of most social media listening tools. However, the best practice is to use it more tactically, with more nuance. For example: asking, "how do you feel about product one versus product two?" or looking deeper into those conversations that are tagged with a neutral sentiment. Sentiment literally reflects the audience's opinions and feelings so it's central to what we're talking about. We suggest this customization because the automated out-of-the-box functionality doesn't completely capture the complexity of sentiment due to the limitations of natural language processing (NLP).

Limitations of NLP. There have been significant advances in NLP. This is why you can "ask" Alexa or Siri things using your natural language style: "what is the weather in New York City today?" as opposed to "Alexa. Weather. Zip code 10012."

But it does have its limitations—you've almost certainly had the experience where things go haywire and Alexa doesn't understand what you meant, because our natural language style is full of idioms and sarcasm and local accents. For example, the machines don't yet know how to grade the sentiment in these two statements:

"This is shit!"

"This is *the* shit!"

The machines will tag the second sentence as negative even though we know as humans that addition of the word "the" means someone is making a positive statement. Therefore, some negative terms may be tagged as negative because NLP can't navigate the context of the negative word. Another example: imagine you received a comment on a storytelling video that you posted with this comment: "Ugh. I'm ugly crying over your video. Even though it made me sad, please keep posting more like this." It's likely that comment would get scored as negative when it's a positive mention!

Sarcasm is also a place for humans to be on the lookout. Imagine you're an airline brand and you get tagged in a tweet saying this: "I love it when [*X airline*] loses my luggage after a ten-hour flight." This isn't a happy customer. But out-of-the-box sentiment scoring may score it that way.

So, humans are still needed to support the NLP tools. And that's why we put so much emphasis on "teams, not tech" with regard to social listening—because NLP has a long way to go.

How sentiment is defined

Let's look at the way sentiment is defined and how it rates conversations positive, neutral, or negative. Social media sentiment analysis applies NLP to analyze online mentions of your "listeners" and determine the feelings behind the content that was posted. Essentially, the algorithms apply NLP and machine learning to public social mentions from various social media sources. Fun fact: social media sentiment analysis is also called opinion mining. (I love it when things come together with a nice, neat bow!)

Sentiment terms, or defining what's positive or negative, can be relatively straightforward. Others might be specific to your industry. Either way, you should define your sentiment terms for both positive and negative. Here are a few common terms and examples:

- **positive sentiment:** best, love, amazing, perfect, thanks
- **negative sentiment:** worst, hate, disappointed, bad, avoid

Negative sentiment is awesome (if you act!)

Now, let's lean in on the negative—because this is where you can seriously initiate change. In my opinion, you start here. During the pandemic, we saw brand loyalty wane even more; brands are losing clients more easily, and by digging into the negative you may be able to improve retention and turn that trend around.

Remember the coffee filter anecdote? Another benefit was that, with negative chatter out of the way, more customers started to praise the product (positive sentiment). Over the six-month period following the release of the video shown in figure 10-1 we saw negative sentiment for this product decrease from 44 percent to 13 percent, which meant positive sentiment rose to 87 percent. Imagine if nearly half your feedback was negative, and six months later it was barely more than 10 percent? Not bad.

And what happens when people are raving about a product on social media? You raise awareness and increase peer-to-peer recommendations. And many times, those positive reactions lead to sales.

If you are looking for acquisition, this is how you find the opportunities to get new customers. The negative feedback is where, if you truly want to become a better brand, you go to make the changes your customers want to see. In some cases, these are the changes they have been begging for. Similarly, you can also look at your competitors' negative sentiment, and find opportunities to differentiate yourself from others in your space. Ignoring negative feedback is not just

Figure 10-1

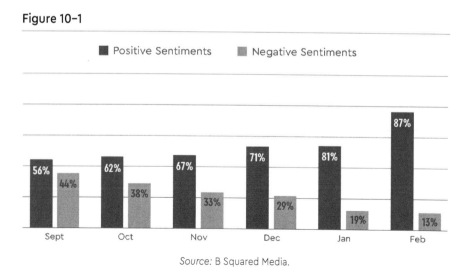

Source: B Squared Media.

bad (terrible!) customer care—it's also such a missed opportunity. Feedback on social media is public—and the rest of the audience can see the feedback *and* your lack of response.

Look at the example in figure 10-2 from the hair care brand Kerastase.[2] Here the user is clearly in pre-purchase (just about to check out) when she reaches out for help on the purchase transaction. And no response from the brand, apparently, because we see her reach out again a week later.

Figure 10-2

Um, if your customers want to buy things . . . help them.

Source: Kerastase (@KerastaseUSA), Twitter.

With 16,000 followers and posts going out multiple times per week, it feels unconscionable to me that they would leave this potential customer hanging out there so long. They literally just left money on the table—not to mention publicly ignored someone.

Here's another example in figure 10-3 from the luxury candle brand Diptyque.³ Yikes! Here is someone who (1) clearly states that they are a past customer, and (2) has even bought this specific

Figure 10-3

Source: Diptyque (@diptyque), Instagram.

fragrance previously. Plus, they even say they'd like to buy it again next year. Why wouldn't the brand reach out? (By the way—these candles are um ... luxury priced. These customers make an investment in home fragrance, and I would guess they expect the brand to listen to them.)

Clients often don't want to look at the negative, and they *really* don't want to look at it and alter the way things are being done. But if you want to institute change, this is where it happens. And nine times out of ten, when you show your customers (1) we're listening to what you said, even though it's negative, and (2) we're making changes based on the opinions and feelings you gave, you'll have an easier time getting their buy-in and hopefully getting them to remain loyal.

By the way, this might be counterintuitive if you're in marketing but, instead of showcasing what people like—the positive—to your stakeholders, you need to be brave and focus on what's not working because that's where there is room to improve. Fun fact: no brand is perfect and there will always be room to grow. Yes, these are tough conversations, but they are the only way to transform your bad mentions into positive ones. And quite possibly, to turn disgruntled customers into loyal ones.

The power of positive sentiment

The positive can also be ... well, positive! As I mentioned previously, this is often where you find user-generated content. Once you see it, you can reach out to that user and ask to re-post on the brand's channels. It's also an opportunity for acquisition: you can mirror the words that are used in positive sentiment when one peer recommends your products or services to another peer.

Positive sentiment can also alert you to how your products are being used differently or highlight consumer innovation. By the way, it can be interesting for brands to learn how their product is being used in an unexpected or unintended way. IKEA product hacks are a good example of this. All you need to do is Google "IKEA product hacks" and there are several sites with several hundreds of hacks customers have provided for their IKEA buys. Now, imagine you are IKEA. Couldn't you have a whole series of content posts about these hacks? Could you start a community around product hacks? The answer is yes. Armed with social media intelligence and social listening data, you can literally go from "here's what people are talking about in relation to our brand" to "here's a community of loyal IKEA customers who help others buy more of our stuff with product hacks." The leap may seem long, but I promise it's easier than you think.

Positive sentiment is also important if you're implementing a strategy for social-led customer care. Don't think of customer support in the old school way (just fix the bad things!); that's focused on retention which is one narrow vertical within your broader engagement. The new way to think about social-led customer care also involves acquisition: which is gained by engaging in positive experiences *and* using those positive experiences in a way that can be leveraged on social media. Companies need to recognize, and take advantage of, how much consumers are influenced by others' recommendations whether it's influencers (those the company pays to promote the brand), or brand advocates (loyal consumers, employee-advocates, etc.).

Positive sentiment: finding advocates and influencers. One little, tiny thing (actually a huge thing but not really the point of this book)—sentiment analysis is great for identifying advocates and influencers. B Squared Media has helped with identifying advocates and influencers for some of our customer care clients by looking at the positive sentiment associated with certain users. This is because we start to become relatively intimate with those who are constantly sharing the brand's praises. This can sometimes be easier or more economical than finding and paying an influencer company. Or it can be a better way of identifying and moving advocates to paid influencers. Sure, these influencers are likely smaller, but you might find a better-connected person who will work harder for you if you first find the advocate and later make her an influencer.

Neutral isn't nothing

Finally, when it comes to neutral sentiment analysis, my advice is to scan it. Should it really be negative or positive? If so, we usually re-tag as such. But mostly, we scan it because it's devoid of emotion, so it's not helpful for sentiment analysis. However, you should ask your team why the specific features of your product are getting a neutral rating. The warning sign here is that if you're seeing lots of neutral sentiment, your brand may be giving off a whole lot of "meh." If you're living in neutral, that's a problem. The good news is this can easily be solved by sharing more (and asking for more) opinions and feelings.

Tracking Sentiment over Time

How do people feel about your brand or your products this week, versus last week? Social media listening allows you to track sentiment in real-time, so it's easy to immediately see if there's a significant change in how much people are talking about you. Or, if the feelings behind what they're saying about you have changed. Think of it like an early warning system. It alerts you to both positive and negative changes in how your brand is perceived through online conversations, in real time. And since we know customers are eager to bash brands online versus commend them, it can be a major indicator that a communications crisis is about to rear its ugly head.

Next Level: Advanced Sentiment Tips

If you're already an expert on sentiment and want to take sentiment data to the next level, here are three ways to measure that:

1. **Frequency.** How often does your customer or would-be customer provide feedback? How often does your customer or would-be customer interact with you on social media?
2. **Volume.** How much time does your customer or would-be customer spend offering feedback? How much time does your customer or would-be customer spend interacting with you on social media?
3. **Overall Score.** Are your customers' or would-be customers' thoughts and feelings mostly positive or negative? Are they neutral? Why?

The wrap-up on executing sentiment—proficiently, I mean, not just executing out-of-the-box analysis—is that when you are fluent in how people feel about your brand it can help you differentiate your brand. When you communicate to the community by showing that you've been listening to what the community said about your product, it's magical. And now you can mirror their actual words in how they describe their sentiment about the product. What they like and why. How they use it, the unique ways in which they use it, etc. You can reflect the emotions and sentiment attached to very specific products/features/uses, etc.—which is something we see so few brands doing today.

Now it's time to discuss how to use metrics to analyze the effectiveness of your conversations that connect. You'll need to be able to measure some of the things we've touched on throughout the book to prove success.

CHAPTER ELEVEN
Metrics and KPIs

Historically, the ability to quantify marketing has been difficult, especially in terms of return on investment (ROI). But with all the social listening platforms and other tools available today you can—and should—measure a lot of your social media intelligence. You can use this data for everything from assessing the performance of team members, to justifying your budget to the C-suite. Obviously, different metrics are useful for different needs. I won't try to tell you which metrics you should use. Knowing which things to measure is personal to your brand and its needs. But I can explain some that are most common, and which ones our clients often find valuable.

Key Performance Indicators

With most of our clients, when it comes to thinking about metrics, we start with understanding company goals first. Our clients come from hugely diverse industries and from very different stages of their digital marketing strategy. But once we understand the goals, we can then help establish key performance indicators (KPIs) that will help show if they are meeting those goals. And then, individual metrics are set that will tell us how and why we are (or are not) meeting the KPIs. Although metrics support KPIs, which help you meet goals, metrics also can help inform them. In other words, metrics help build better metrics—you readjust your KPIs and business goals, based on what you see in your metrics. That sounded like a lot, but it's straightforward. I'm going to walk you through it.

Your KPIs should determine your metrics. First, there are literally countless KPIs that can help you measure the success of your social media initiatives. While I can't tell you what your KPIs or your metrics should be, I can tell you that I recommend understanding goals, then setting KPIs, before deciding the metrics. As the adage goes, what gets measured is what gets done, and I think your goals should determine what gets measured. If a KPI for you is improving initial response time to thirty minutes or less on weekdays, and one hour or less on nights and weekends, then the metrics you need are obvious. (There is a whole lot more nuance to responses that I think you should consider, but more on that in a minute.)

KPIs should address potholes. Remember how I told you to look at the digital customer journey and find potholes? And to tag negative sentiment because it's probably pointing to potholes? You should be measuring both the sentiment itself ("How often does someone complain about our checkout process?") and what the problem is ("Why does payment via PayPal seem to cause problems?"). Then, your goal should be to reduce PayPal-based complaints, and the KPI can be to get beneath a specific number of complaints.

Important Metrics

Even though KPIs should inform your metrics, I do think some metrics are just basic foundational numbers to know. This is especially true if you're just getting started. No matter what, you should be customer centric, so your metrics should reflect the flywheel and how you create and sustain the momentum (keeping current customers, how customers become advocates). It's hard to know specifics when you're getting started—like whether you can reply to every inbound within thirty minutes—if you don't know how many inbounds you get and when they come in. But that kind of basic volume metric is important for everyone. You also may want metrics that help you assess your operations. For example, what if you measure how often an inbound requires escalation to a manager or bringing in another department? This might give you an opportunity to create better playbooks for the customer care frontline members.

Volume

There are several different ways to look at volume. Obviously, at its most basic, we're talking about the number of messages (or posts or tweets)—whether outgoing from the brand (outbound) or incoming from your audience (inbound). But you want to know those numbers. If you post a lot (outbound) but have very little inbound, then your content isn't getting much engagement (or the algorithms are preventing it from reaching your followers). Conversely, if you have a lot of inbound, but not much outbound, are you responding to everyone? If not, that's a big problem. Here is a bit more detail on how to measure volume:

- **Outbound volume.** At its most basic, outbound volume is all the messages you are sending out on all your social media channels. That could be a post, a response, anything that is from the brand. We'll get into some fundamental metrics related to your outbound messages in a minute.
- **Inbound volume.** The number of incoming messages on all social media channels is inbound volume. My advice here is to calculate the percentage of customer service issues compared to the total number of social inbound messages that are *not* related to customer support. This will help you make decisions regarding a social-led customer care strategy.
- **Response volume.** Response volume is technically outgoing content published by your brand, but it's in response to inbound messages. If this number is vastly lower than your inbound volume your brand is not likely doing a good job of being perceived as a stellar brand on social media, because (as I've said before!) your audience expects you to be responding to messages. We'll go into more detail on response

metrics—but the absolute most basic baseline is to at least know the volume.
- **Volume by category.** Your number of messages by interaction type or tag/label types is your volume by category. As discussed earlier, you can include broad categories such as marketing messages, public relations messages, or customer support messages (i.e., tags). You're likely to include subcategories or tags/labels within these, such as issues related to products/services, deliveries, website, or app, etc.

Outbound metrics

Just measuring the basic outbound volume isn't very nuanced. I recommend you have some additional related metrics that will give you a 360-degree view of your social media performance. Since these are relatively standard, I'll give the definition of each and then move on.

1. **Impressions.** Impressions represent the number of times your content is shown to users, no matter if they clicked on it or not.
2. **Reach.** Reach is the number of unique people who see your content. If twenty-five individual people each viewed your content twice, reach would be twenty-five. But impressions would be fifty.
3. **Engagement rates.** Engagement rates are how well your content is received by your audience. When consumers are engaged, they typically interact with brands through "likes," reactions, comments, and social sharing.

Social media share of voice

This measures a brand's exposure based on social media conversations. It's usually measured among a defined group of competitors. You can calculate your share of voice (SOV) using the formula in figure 11-1.

Figure 11-1

$$X / Y \times 100 = SOV$$

X *(number of mentions in a given time period for your brand)* **/ Y** *(the total number of brand mentions (yours + your competitors') in a given time period)* **x 100 = Share of Voice**

Source: B Squared Media.

Measuring Response Times

First, before we get into what is the right response time on social media, it's worth saying no response is unacceptable. That might sound obvious, but a survey by ResultsCX found that more than half (52 percent) of respondents interacted with a brand on social media for a question or concern.[1] Of those, 19 percent said they did not receive any feedback. No answer at all? Imagine walking into a store and asking for help and no one answering? Seriously?

If your brand is tagged (@ mentioned), you should be responding as quickly as you can. HubSpot research showed that 79 percent of customers in 2021 expect a response to their social media posts within twenty-four hours.[2] That's reasonable (though many companies still struggle to do this, especially on weekends). But the harsher reality is that 39 percent of social media users expect a response within *sixty minutes*—and the average response time for businesses is about *five hours*. So, even though 63 percent of social media complaints are responded to within twenty-four hours, only 32 percent of people are happy with their response time. *Your target response time should be one hour* (or close to that)—not twenty-four.

In fact, a one-hour window might even be too generous. Yep—the ResultsCX survey found that 38 percent of respondents believe a brand's social media account should respond within fifteen minutes and 34 percent believe the response time should be "instant."[3] While research and surveys vary on the response time expected from brands on social media, the consumer expectation is clear: show up, and do it *quickly*.

In today's (online) reality, you're in a competition twenty-four seven. Brand loyalty is up for grabs; it's cagey, waning, and customer retention is critical. Get this straight: If you're not taking the time to answer, no answer *is* your answer. You're both giving and eliciting feelings whether you know it or not and not answering says you couldn't care less about your potential and current customers. From their side, I'm sure the feeling will be mutual. Not only that, with social media you have spectators. Whether you answer quickly, or not at all, you're telling onlookers how to define your brand.

Your prospects and customers *expect* to have conversations with you. They expect you to engage, respond, and interact. Not every comment or mention needs a response, but even a simple "like" on someone's comment can show that you're listening.

Define response time KPIs. I hope there's one tiny thing you've come away with from this book and that is responding is a given. (Empathy also should be a given.) But response time goals require that you reflect on what you can realistically offer and how to improve that. For example, what can you provide with consistency? One client of ours set a KPI of a ten-minute initial response time from our team to acknowledge the customer and then triage the next steps. And while our team was able to meet this KPI, the client's internal customer support team often took days, sometimes weeks, to follow up on any escalated "red" issues.

This became a real point of annoyance for their customers. I feel like I need to reiterate that consumers aren't dumb; soon these customers realized that they were getting a ten-minute initial response on social media, but it was taking days or weeks for the internal team to follow up with a solution. We started getting "re-escalations" on social—meaning people were saying that they requested something from internal support ten days ago and still haven't gotten a response. When internal response times didn't improve, it turned from confusion to anger, and the brand was constantly being scolded for not being as quick with actual problem resolution as our team (their professional provider) was with initial response. All of this to say, and caution, that your social-led conversations and support should match what you're capable of doing internally. You can absolutely set a ten-minute KPI for initial response times, which is well below what most consumers expect for response times on social media. But if you set up that expectation, you may be setting yourself up for failure on the ultimate resolution timeline. (As an aside, the client ended up pushing out our social media response time goal to ninety minutes. But that didn't solve the lag time on ultimate resolution of escalated issues.)

As I've mentioned before, customer support on social media is not the same as a traditional customer support helpline, and people have very different expectations when it comes to response times. People are accustomed to a telephone line being only available during traditional business hours. They might even anticipate that an email they send at two a.m. won't get a response until the next day. But as I pointed out above, when consumers reach out to a brand via social media, they want a response within an hour. That includes the folks who reach out at eleven p.m. on a Saturday night.

And remember my very early example about the broken button problem on social media—companies quickly have two problems: first is whatever the consumer is complaining about. Second is taking two days to reply. At our technology brand client, they had a third problem—by not responding to complaints over the weekend, they had a pile up of requests Monday morning that took them nearly two days to get through. So, if you sent a complaint on a Saturday morning, it didn't get read until at least first thing Monday, and if you wrote later in the weekend, it could be late Tuesday before you heard back. This is why at B Squared Media we put an emphasis on quick turnarounds for responding (and we offer 365-day coverage, so you don't have that Monday morning pileup).

Let's dive into how we measure response times and more on the following pages.

Response and Resolution

We've already discussed how important it is to respond. But it's different to merely reply, as opposed to resolving the user's problem. In fact, merely replying—without solving the problem—is not only inadequate, but it can also be maddening for a customer! Responses are therefore more nuanced and effective metrics should make a distinction. Here is a further breakdown of different response metrics:

Response rate or average reply time. The average reply time is simply the average time a customer must wait for an initial response. It's the time from receiving a customer message to the moment a reply is sent, and then dividing that number by the number of customer messages.

Response times and time to resolution. Response times, and time to resolution, can be broken down into (1) *first touch response*, and (2) *time to resolution*. First touch response (also called first touch resolution) is the time it takes to answer any inbound message. It's the rate at which requests are resolved without needing to defer to a future date or escalate the request. When we do have to escalate, we must separately track their time to resolve the issue—that is the *time to resolution*. So, it's both first touch response time plus the time to resolution that we are measuring. In the previous example, while the client set a KPI for a ten-minute first touch response (great!), the time to resolution was as long as seventeen days (definitely not great).

Sentiment Metrics

As we've discussed, sentiment analysis looks at the conversations and applies a label of positive, neutral, or negative.

Negative sentiment. Our biggest use of negative sentiment analysis is identifying the potholes. You have tagged negative sentiment, and now you review those metrics. Obviously wherever your metrics show high negative sentiment, you probably have a pothole.

Customer satisfaction. Customer satisfaction, or CSAT, is a measurement of how happy people are with your product or service. It is estimated through survey forms filled out by customers after interacting with your support team. To calculate the CSAT, divide the number of positive responses by the number of total responses and multiply it by 100.

Net promoter score. Net promoter score (NPS) represents the percentage of customers who recommend a company, a product, or a service to their peers based on their perception of a business. Companies usually have three categories of customers: promoters, passives, and detractors. To calculate the NPS score, take the percentage of promoters (9–10) and subtract the percentage of detractors (0–6).

- **Promoters.** Your loyal customer base who rated you between nine and ten are promoters.
- **Passives.** Satisfied customers (passive customers) are those who feel improvement can be done and often rate you between seven and eight.

- **Detractors.** Unhappy customers are detractors—those who would likely discourage their peers from buying from your company. These people rate you below seven.

Measuring Brand Mentions

Most companies will track in their customer relationship management system (CRM) who their high value clients are by revenue. Metrics could help you go further by mining those people for advocates (people who both are high value and are online a lot). For example, you could use them to help you build a community. Ask those high value customers, who also are highly engaged in your social media conversations, to be community leaders.

Remember cat mom Kristy, who received a surprise and delight gift from Chewy? I would think (suggest!) that they tracked how many times Kristy mentioned the brand and tagged her as a high value customer. Note that I mean this from a social media potential perspective, not just high revenue (every brand has customers who purchase a lot but don't promote the brand on social media). I'd also tag the actual act of sending the gift—make a record that you gave the gift to Kristy as a surprise and delight initiative. If she had then posted the picture on her social media, I would expect the brand to ask to share that user-generated content on their channels. All this both helps retain her loyalty as well as hopefully prompt her to create her own content. These kinds of things are not as transactional in nature so you won't be able to quantify an immediate ROI, but it's usually a good investment in the long run so you'd want to be tracking metrics on this. You should note how much that campaign cost versus how much UGC it garnered ("we spent this much giving it to ten people and nine people mentioned it on social media").

UGC metrics. Speaking of UGC, this is another metric that I suggest you track. Regarding conversations that connect, I think what you'll begin to see is certain conversation triggers result in

UGC. So, you should have a system for identifying which types of content inspire UGC. And then of course, start creating more of that kind of content.

Finding the Right Tools for Your Metrics

Of course, there are many amazing tools for social media metrics. A few that I've had good experiences with include Talkwalker, Emplifi, and Mention. Some are less expensive, and others are a larger investment but offer more expansive tools. Google Alerts, for instance, is extremely basic, but free. Mention is a paid service (but has a free plan that allows for one social listening alert). Based on your needs, goals, and budget, you'll want to ensure you find the right tool for you. And if you really want the goods, shoot me a message (see Additional Resources) and I'll let you know more about which ones we love. And which ones we try to stay away from.

At B Squared Media, we use Sprout Social, and find that their "inbox team report" is particularly beneficial when you have several people dedicated to providing social support through the tool's "smart inbox." The report breaks down reply metrics by team member, so each person can remain informed of, and accountable for, their performance. This is one of the many things you may want to ask about if you're going to demo social media dashboards and listening tools. The more they do for you, the easier your job will be to reach your shared goals.

CHAPTER TWELVE
Teams, Not Tech

I hope that you're now convinced of just how important it is to have conversations that connect! And how to identify your audience. Also, why Negative Nancys are your friend. And how to think about metrics. Plus, why social-led customer care is critical. Umm . . . that's a lot, and you're going to need a team to do it—let's talk about how to build those resources. The right team is incredibly important. And because so much of this space of social media is new (and evolving constantly!), getting the right team isn't easy.

First, there are two obvious options—build a team in-house or bring in a professional provider who can partner with you. There are advantages to each, as there are with almost any function you choose to manage directly or outsource.

Outsourcing social-led customer care (and conversations that connect!), can help your brand scale quickly because it comes packaged with structure, tools, and processes in place. And it's cheaper; our entire team and service usually costs less than one or two experienced full-time employees. As an outsourced partner, we have huge resources, expertise, and experience in managing social-led support for brands of all different sizes and industries. This means you can expect to have a modern social CX plan from the get-go.

It's important to note though, that outsourcing is not for everyone. It requires a keen understanding of your specific needs so you can ensure the alignment of those needs with the capabilities of your outsourced partner. That's the only way objectives are met. The whole "I don't know what I want but I'll know it when I see it" attitude won't work. At B Squared Media, we customize our social-led customer care services to a company's values and needs. This strategy helps us reflect the brand while they also can leverage the benefits of outsourcing.

I'll detail in the following pages the considerations on both sides of this choice so you can make the right decision for your brand.

Should We Do This In-House or Use a Professional Provider?

I know what you're thinking: "here comes the sales pitch for using B Squared Media." Not quite (though we're happy to chat with you about how to help!). What I want to do is help you think through what you need, and why it might be more efficient to at least start with a professional provider (even if it's not us). I want to highlight some things to consider when you're deciding about how to put a team against the various things we've discussed here.

By the way, I understand how it can be difficult to get buy-in to invest in an outside resource: so also consider the following to make your case to the C-suite. My friend and client Jill Sammons, senior vice president of marketing & strategic communications at BCU, said it took three years to retain outside services: "In 2015, we knew we needed to use social media in a different way but couldn't get buy-in . . . until 2018. And this was after trying to DIY it!"

I totally get this. It's hard to wrap your head around something this new, with so many moving pieces—you just read a couple hundred pages on how many things you must keep in mind. I am not saying you can't take pieces of this in-house. And you can certainly transition over time—any outside provider worth their salt should be happy to help you build up your capabilities.

Things to consider when building a team in-house

Knowhow. First, this is a new space that's in constant evolution. No one has been doing social-led customer care for twenty years!

But with a professional provider, you do get the benefit of all the ways we've done it, with dozens of clients, across all kinds of industries. Part of being an expert in this field is staying up to date with the newest trends (I don't mean fads—I mean best practices, benchmarks, etc.), resources, changes in the industry, and synthesizing all that information into processes. Not only do we have the tools and people in place, but we also have the time in the trenches—we can save you an enormous amount of time by avoiding things we've seen that just didn't work. Lots of very smart marketers have made very rational decisions about how to approach this space and learned the hard way when something didn't work. (Sometimes those very smart marketers were us. Lesson learned.) We can save you a lot of that time. We need to get to know your specific business, pain points and goals, but we don't have to reinvent the wheel—we've been driving around for more than a decade!

Cost. One of the most obvious costs is headcount. As I'm sure you know, every full-time employee (FTE) costs more than just salary—an individual on an annual salary of $50,000 can cost you $60,000–70,000 in total benefits and taxes (the Small Business Association estimates that the actual cost of an employee is 1.2–1.4 times the salary).[1] On average, you can get full service, multi-member, 365-day coverage with B Squared Media for less than two FTEs. But, of course, there's also the cost of time—to recruit, onboard, train, and manage employees. And keep in mind that social-led customer care requires staffing for nights, weekends, and holidays. This inevitably increases the cost of headcount.

Scale and flexibility. One of the advantages of a dedicated agency is that they can scale up or down to meet your needs. With social-led customer care, that can be particularly useful, especially when you're first getting started. As you engage in social listening and then begin to build an audience, your needs will be hard to predict and prone to change. When you move into social-led customer care (I'm assuming you will—aren't you convinced?!), your needs in terms of volume and scope will also be fluid. One of our clients said that's a key advantage of an outside agency. Jill Sammons at BCU, told me the following: "The goalposts are always moving and it's good that we don't have to keep up with that. For example, what are the most critical coverage times—sometimes it's seven p.m. on Friday and then it's Tuesday at three a.m."

As I mentioned earlier, FTEs are expensive, and if your staffing needs fluctuate, it can be difficult to ramp up and down. We've discussed knowing your audience and thinking about seasonality trends for your brand. But with social media, things outside of your control can also cause a surge of activity. For example, brands like Home Depot and Lowe's almost certainly see a surge of activity when there is a natural disaster. But that's impossible to predict—if a surge of users begin to ask about a snowplow or generators, they will need answers urgently.

Integration: how to include customer care, everywhere

When it comes to social-led customer care—the way I have articulated it in this book—it's a pretty radical departure from the way most brands approach their digital marketing *or* their traditional customer support. This could mean a fairly significant reorganization of your teams. Depending on how large you are, that can impact everything from which budget it hits to reporting lines to skill set mismatches. For example, if you have outsourced customer support to a call center, they are probably too isolated from stakeholders in your company for the integration that true customer care requires. They also are unlikely to have social media capabilities. In fact, we make it clear with our clients that we will not be replacing call center or email support teams. Social-led customer care is a completely different animal (but of course you know that now!).

Building a Customer Care Team In-House

If you're keen on doing it in-house, I've got a few tips for you on how to organize your team. And then we'll talk about the skills they'll need and other considerations.

First, if your customer care team is in-house, they need to be integrated with decision makers in other departments. For example, who can they reach out to in sales when someone has a pre-purchase question they can't answer? What about when they field a question about a technical glitch as opposed to a product question—will someone from IT be able to take over? These kinds of questions ideally need to be resolved as soon as possible. Remember those response timelines we mentioned above, and the client where our team made an initial response within ten minutes, but it was taking days to get the problem resolved? That won't cut it.

Another integration need that is less immediate but still urgent—you can cut down on negative sentiment by resolving the underlying problems that cause the potholes. Remember the finance client who fixed their cashback app? And the coffee brand who created a YouTube how-to video? You want to have a process where you can give feedback to other departments that can make a lasting change that resolves it. And don't forget to have the customer care team then broadcast that resolution: remember Blume, the cosmetics brand that changed the packaging to a dropper? They were able to generate tons of positive sentiment when they announced they had not only heard, but heeded, user feedback.

Team structure

How you organize your different social media team roles is also critical. Your hierarchy should outline who takes the lead during different scenarios and promote a culture of accountability. Creating a structure of team leaders and managers helps identify the decision-maker with varying deliverables. This will come in handy when you have escalations. In rare cases, we've seen where several internal managers were needed to resolve complex cases (and this often leads to process or documentation iterations). My golden-nugget piece of advice is to make it crystal clear who is in charge of what. When you have a situation where two people are unclear of who is in charge, it leads to conflict or stagnation. "I thought so-and-so was doing it," won't help you in a crisis.

When it comes to setting up your team, I can't tell you what's best for you. You'll have to decide that on your own. Or, if you select us to be your professional provider (yes, please!) that's something we can work on together. What I can do is give you a glimpse into how we set up our structure—but keep in mind, as an agency, we are dealing with many clients in many different industries, so you may need to modify your structure since you are likely servicing only one company or brand. Here's how the B² Crew is structured:

Chief service officer. We added the chief service officer (CSO) role in July 2021 when my husband came onboard (hi, Alex!). More than likely, for you, this will be your CMO, marketing or product vice president, or customer service leader—or a combination of those people. As CSO, Alex is responsible for managing service initiatives related to the people, products, and processes of B Squared Media. He's also accountable for optimizing service technology and operations for the greatest benefits in profit margin, customer retention, and revenue growth. You may also consider a customer experience officer (CXO) as an alternative. The CXO is responsible for the entire customer journey, including the digital customer journey.

Project manager. Our entire social-led customer care operation is headed by our project manager (PM), sometimes called a director. With our setup, this person reports to the CEO (me) and the CSO. They make strategic decisions, oversee the budget, manage client KPIs, coordinate the shift schedule, and manage documentation for each of our projects. The PM is the team leader, so they also handle routine and administrative decisions like prioritizing client deliverables and monitoring weekly performance (team side and client side).

Account manager. Account managers (AMs) oversee operational and tactical decisions. At B Squared Media, AMs are assigned to specific client accounts. In house, you might only need one AM, or if you have a large portfolio of products, you may want to assign them by product line. AMs are responsible for critical areas such as developing a team roster (i.e., which team member will best serve each brand), sketching out workflows and processes, and acting as the main point of contact for client counterparts. Specifically, our AMs are responsible for the social listening components that go with their respective client accounts, including the set-up, ongoing management, and reporting. They also disseminate the reports and findings to the client (which can include customer support team members, all the way up to the CMO). Our AMs also manage our community managers.

Community managers. Most of our staff is made up of our frontline agents, also called community managers (CMGRs). These team members man the frontline, monitoring and responding to acquisition or retention support requests that come in on each of the social media channels we're managing. For us, they work on certain clients/brands on a shift schedule. For you, they could be organized by channel or product/service type.

Other hierarchy considerations

The organizational structure you choose will involve the roles you have in place currently to accomplish the stated objectives, and the dynamic of relationships among positions. When figuring out your own hierarchy, there are many things to consider. Your organization's structure should be designed to identify an effective framework:

- Who does what (and who is ultimately responsible for results)?
- Which team member is responsible for removing obstacles to performance (many times this is caused by the lack of documentation or disorganization of the documentation I laid out in Chapter Eight: Social-Led Customer Care)?
- Who is the decision-maker and thereby the person responsible for communicating changes to the team?

The channels you choose for social support services will determine other important factors like response volume, agent expertise needed, shift scheduling, and predictability of outcomes. All these should influence how you structure your team.

Because social-led customer care is an "inbound" function, it will require a thoughtful hierarchy to handle escalation. Escalation, as we touched on earlier, is what happens when the person handling your social inbox cannot answer on their own with a solution. In this scenario, CMGRs often need backup to help them manage the tougher inquiries. As I mentioned earlier, inbound social-led operations require a knowledge base to facilitate FAQs.

The Social Support Skillset

From a 30,000-foot view, the team members responsible for having conversations that connect, collecting data, and measuring it all will be vital to your success. In addition to understanding the technology, the various social media platforms, and some of the foundational measures we're talking about in this book, your social team needs to have some serious writing skills. What's more, when (notice I didn't say *if*) your social team gets that complicated support task, it will pay off immensely to have someone who can clearly articulate how to solve the problem. So, communication with context is a must-have skill, as is organization. I'd rather have one social media agent or community manager who can do all the above and prove the value of social media to our clients than ten who can post the perfect meme. Trust me, I've learned this the hard way!

Additionally, a customer support background is massively helpful. This doesn't necessarily mean this person has been a social care agent. Customer support experience can include anything from a hospitality background to working in retail.

Jaime, our project manager who currently oversees our social-led customer care team, worked at a Montessori school as a director of admissions before finding her way to us. She has her master's in education administration. Though admissions technically is a "sales" job, Jaime always considered it more educational than anything else. And let's be honest, dealing with parents (and kids) is an excellent way to up your customer service game! Jaime brought these educational skills to us along with her calm-under-pressure leadership, organization, and follow-through. I'm certain that her admissions career now helps her navigate the sometimes-murky waters of customer care.

When it comes to intangible skills, during hiring, you'll want to look for those who are customer-centric, who exercise good judgment and exhibit buckets of empathy! You'll know this when they go the extra mile to help a team member; as Mister Rogers said: "look for the helpers"—the tutors, the volunteers, the teachers. We've found that hiring people who are actively involved in charity make great social-led care agents. The tech can be taught. Intrinsic values cannot.

Speaking of teaching the tech, I teach a digital marketing certificate course for a billion-dollar scientific brand that introduces their employees to the fundamentals of marketing. The students are located around the globe, and the brand does this so that there is a universal understanding of how to approach their marketing strategy. They appreciate that building out an in-house team means not only understanding the core products and services, but really investing in the team's fluency in marketing and the accompanying technology.

CX = Care

Let's assume you already have social media or community managers who are quite capable of leading the charge for social support. To ready your own teams for the uptick in social-led customer care you must ensure they have a broad understanding of customer experience across multiple customer touchpoints. Make sure you have a plan for delivering a consistent experience for each touchpoint in your digital journey, including options for customer support and those who are on the path to purchase.

To do it well, social media customer experience teams should be in constant communication with all teams—but without loss of autonomy as your first line of defense. Autonomy is what allows decisions to be made faster and cheaper.

To verify your social-led customer care team has a keen eye for CX as they operate day-to-day, have them notate when and why certain outcomes happen along the digital customer journey. Here are some ways to learn and improve the DCJ:

- "Shop" your own social-led customer support from the customer's point of view. (We have a secret social shopper service that can help you do this! More on that in Resources.)
- Note how customers interact with each of your digital touchpoints.
- Document your wins and moments of pain (what's working and what isn't).
- Create goals to overcome the "potholes" (gaps) and highlight the opportunities along the digital journey.

Don't be afraid of an overhaul of your digital journey if you find more bad than good.

I can imagine at this point that your eyes are starting to water from all that goes into a successful social-led customer care program. Tackling this in-house operation is not only strenuous, but it can also be costly. As I pointed out in the beginning of the book, the fundamental structure of organizations, and the requirements of social media-based customer support, are simply an inherent mismatch. Trying to scale on your own can limit your capacity to expand or improve.

CHAPTER THIRTEEN
Final Feelings

As marketers, we are intimately familiar with CX. The definition of CX is the experience your customers have at the sum of all touchpoints with your brand. With conversations that connect, we should aim to invoke feelings at every touchpoint. That way, by the end of your brand's digital customer journey, you will have invoked feelings, which lead to (hopefully excellent) memories, which lead to how the customer feels about your brand. And since the customer is now in control, and they ultimately decide what your brand is, those memories inform what defines your brand; how your customer tells others about your brand.

To wrap up, I'm going to revisit the question of "where do we start?". First, reading this book was a good start, I hope! What you do next somewhat depends on where your brand is currently.

Getting Started

If now you're convinced that it's time to invest in your social media strategy (yay!), I recommend you start with these steps:

- **Accept that social is skyrocketing.** It's key to remember that you need to be leaning into the power of social media. The trend toward online shopping and relying on social media to make shopping decisions, has skyrocketed since the pandemic. That is not going to change.
- **Know your DCJ.** Figure out the digital customer journey for your brand. Fix the potholes, and you'll improve CX and increase brand loyalty. It will help you find your users so that

you can build your audience. Identifying where you have the most or the best conversations with your audiences and community will tell you where to spend most of your time.

- **Listen, learn, and take the lead.** The importance of social media listening cannot be overstated. The brand winners are paying attention to customer needs, analyzing those insights, and adapting accordingly. Get good at social media listening—not just social monitoring—this will be a gold mine of information. Who is talking about you, what they are saying, why they do (or don't) choose your products or services? You want to observe the current conversations, before you jump in. Quick tip: I partnered with Sprout Social to create a free accompanying workbook *Social Listening Step-By-Step: How to Revolutionize the Way You Connect, Converse, and Convert* (See Appendix Resources for the link!). It can help you nail down social listening in ninety minutes.

- **Know that negative customer feedback is a superpower.** Sure, the positive mentions and glowing reviews are great and all, but the real space for change lies in the negative. Customer data, including social media intelligence, is a strategic advantage for all brands. Developing stronger relationships through improved (not even amazing) customer experiences is one of the most effective ways to accelerate growth and revenue.

- **It's not ABC, it's SPT.** You must get out of the mindset of "always be closing." You must connect before you can convert. Instead, use the social penetration theory to help you with everything from your initial connections to building conversations that connect. You should also be less focused on the channel. The platform is not the point. If you have great conversations, you will build relationships, improve the DCJ, and deliver a stellar CX—which, again, is the way to create brand loyalty.

If you want help getting started, you might benefit from some initial direction from a professional. For example, our "social media mystery shop" can secretly shop your brand to see how you measure up against your KPIs. Our community managers shop one of your platforms, and then provide a report that measures how your social team and brand performed, and shares insights for improvement. Things we address include: Are your social interactions measuring up to your customer's expectations? Are the customers receiving quick, painless, and helpful interactions? Is your team armed with consistent answers and following your well thought out KPIs? See Appendix: Resources for more about this service.

If You're Ready for the Next Level

Were you already clear on your digital customer journey? Fantastic—have you also identified the potholes? What are you doing to fix them? If you know your DCJ *and* utilize social media listening to help you understand who and where your audiences are, even better.

Commit to a customer-care mindset. Ideally, you want to be doing all those things and also gathering social media intelligence—and not just for the marketing department. This data should be shared across the organization so that everyone can make better data-driven decisions. In fact, you should push yourselves to make customer care part of the corporate culture. In a customer-centric world (which is where we now live . . . welcome), your social media intelligence can and should inform most of your decisions. If you think back to examples in this book, customers gave feedback on everything from packaging (expensive serums should be dispensed by dropper, not pump) to what kind of how-to guides should be on YouTube (changing a coffee filter on a luxury machine). Our jewelry brand didn't just learn who was buying their products—it made them rethink which new items to introduce, where to build the next store, and what kind of ad spend to implement. Your C-suite needs to be bought in, because doing this right is a top-down commitment.

Metrics. Historically, marketing has struggled when pushed to quantify their results. But today's tools (I've listed my suggestions in Appendix: Resources) are immensely helpful: you can (and should) decide what your KPIs are in this space. I can't tell you what to prioritize without being on the ground with you, but I recommend you think about the "why" and "how" not the "what." Why are people buying your product (quality, price, lack of options)? How are they finding out about your brand (our channels, your resellers, third party channels)? Why is your Facebook content not performing as well as your Instagram content (wrong platform for your audience or wrong type of content for that platform)?

Community. Not every brand needs a community, but if you can build one, they will create momentum that you can leverage. IKEA has an entire cottage industry based on people who basically hack their products to turn them into something else. Apple has bona fide artists developing their work on Apple products (but, I mean, they're Apple . . .). But you don't have to be that unique to build and benefit from a community. It just takes time, and lots of listening, and lots of relationship building. If building a community is important to you, and you're beyond some of the basics, there's no shortage of next level steps to take with advocates and influencers. The DCJ is a flywheel because at its best, customers generate more customers and community is a great way to do that. UGC is free—the path to get there is not. But the IKEA community (shown here in figure 13-1 customizing the company's Billy bookcase) is pretty much the holy grail.[1]

If you've gotten many of the fundamentals out of the way, you might want to consider some additional insights on where to improve next. Our "care squared training program" is centered around all the concepts in this book, including the proven processes that we've created and implemented with global, enterprise brands. This offers

Figure 13-1

An enthusiastic community can become an army of customers creating UGC and promoting your products. Yes, please.

Source: YouTube, IKEA channel.

brands who want to DIY their social-led customer care efforts that opportunity while not having to recreate the wheel (or answer the elusive question of "where do we start").

And if you find your internal resources simply can't meet the needs of your audience, this might be the time for partial or full support from a dedicated agency. The case studies in this book come from our real clients—and if you feel you could benefit, then check out our customer care services. Our team of professional community managers engages with your audiences, community, and customers online with authentic, empathetic conversations. Professionally managed social-led customer care not only increases your chances of being seen as a CX leader, but it's also one of the only services that helps your company both acquire and retain customers. Our services ensure that you are there, 365 days a year (yep, even on holidays!). Again, for more information, please see the Appendix: Resources section.

Consumers are Looking for More Connection, Not Content

If you're already sold on social listening and customer care, then I hope you also now understand the power of the SPT and how those feelings and opinions will lead to conversations that connect. I know that's a little bit radical, and it's not easy to implement. I encourage you to challenge yourself to incorporate these final principles into how you build your brand and connect with your audiences. You may have to tear down a few walls and break through traditional thinking to truly achieve this.

The contradictory theme of social media is that it's part of the reason we're so disconnected. The explosion in technology has thrust us into digital transformation over and over, and it seems to get faster and faster each time. And yet, we are looking to this very same medium to come back together, have those conversations that connect, and feel engaged with like-minded people.

Consumers now weigh the *experience* with your brand higher than your product or service. In fact, 80 percent of customers say the experience a company provides is as important as its product or services.[2] I've said multiple times in this book, and I will say it again ... we need less content, more care through conversation. Yet CMOs across the globe spend more time on content, year after year. Forty-three percent of marketers familiar with company spending say their 2021 content marketing budgets were higher than in 2020. And two-thirds of this group (66 percent) expect increases in the 2022 budget. One in five says the increase in the budget will be greater than 9%.³ But people aren't starved for content, they're starved for connection.

Social media and social-led customer care shouldn't be viewed as "just" a cost center. It's not just about spending dollars here versus there. This is more than an argument about economic efficiency. A million dollars spent on the brand community or social-led customer care may yield better ROI than a million on print ads. These conversations—the ones that truly connect—help far more extensively throughout the organization than just customer support. It's providing soft advertising, learning what your competitors are doing well (or not), informing R&D, researching brick-and-mortar location data, and so much more. And having these conversations requires an ongoing dialogue where the brand shares its feelings and opinions and gets the same from its audience. It won't happen overnight; you've got to do the deep work. Steve Jobs once said what I've been trying to say in this entire book: "You've got to start with the customer experience and work backward to the technology. You can't start with the technology then try to figure out where to sell it."⁴ Social media at its core is a type of technology. It is the medium, not the message. Figure out which messages your customers want.

We are consistently overinvested in content marketing and advertising, and not enough in customer care—where the connection is. Yet many brands don't even give people a simple response on social media. If you aren't doing that—the absolute basics—I urge you to get off social media altogether. You're just a noise generator. You need to make way for those of us who really try to care, want to innovate, and strive to make a difference. We want to connect, to inspire, to share our feelings and opinions. We want to tell our stories and know our customers and understand what they want. We know that we don't deserve their loyalty, but we're willing to earn it. We are going to have conversations that connect.

I hope you'll join us.

Appendix: Resources

Social Listening Tools

Google Alerts

Don't forget about Google Alerts, which is free and can serve as a starting point if you're not ready to invest in more robust software. It's primitive at best but will allow you to keep an eye on when your brand is mentioned. (https://www.google.com/alerts)

Mention

Mention is another tool that allows you to monitor online mentions of your brand (and other elements). It offers a free plan with one alert, which you could use to monitor a brand keyword. (https://mention.com)

Sprout Social

At B Squared Media we use Sprout Social for most of our social listening, including reporting and advanced analytics. If you don't already know Sprout Social, I highly encourage you to consider their tools. (https://sproutsocial.com)

Talkwalker

My friend, and trusted analytics partner over at Trust Insights, Christopher Penn, suggests Talkwalker for more sophisticated social listening. He did a great write up on his site with more details. While

I haven't used it personally, I trust Chris and recommend you check it out. (https://www.talkwalker.com)

Additional Resources

Hug Your Haters by Jay Baer

I can't recommend *Hug Your Haters* enough. If you need more convincing that learning to love your Negative Nancys is critical, Jay will do it!

Trust Insights

If you need help with your data and analytics, tracking campaigns, and other initiatives throughout your DCJ, both Christopher Penn and Katie Robbert at Trust Insights are friends and partners we trust. They also have a plethora of free and paid advice on Google Analytics. You can find them at https://www.trustinsights.ai.

Social Listening Step-By-Step: Revolutionize the Way You Connect, Converse, and Convert in 90 Minutes (the workbook)

I hope you enjoyed the book! If you're ready to take social listening to the next level, I encourage you to check out the accompanying workbook that I produced with Sprout Social—it's free! You can get more information at https://bsquared.media/conversations-that-connect-book.

B Squared Media

Obviously, our team at B Squared Media would love to help you! We're always happy to give you a (free!) consultation (we call it a conversation) to understand your needs, and then we'll give you an honest assessment of whether we're the right fit and why. Here are some ways we support our favorite brands:

- **Social Media Mystery Shop.** Our professional community managers will "shop" your online channels to see how your team is currently handling those acquisition or retention requests.
- **Social Listening.** Helping you find those conversations that connect. Everything from identifying your audience and the right channels to brand sentiment, etc.
- **Consulting.** If you're not sure what you need but want a practitioner to guide you through things, you can always book one-on-one time with me!
- **Care Squared Training Program.** If you want to keep your social-led customer care in house but want someone to shepherd your social team through the initial set up, we've got you covered.
- **Social-Led Customer Care.** Let our team of professional community managers handle those holiday and weekend replies that need to be personalized and prompt.

To review all our services, visit https://bsquared.media.

Afterword: How to Support This Book

I'd like to give a Texas-sized hat tip to Melanie Deziel (@mdeziel on Twitter) for realizing I needed this afterword. I spent the better part of twelve years collecting the knowledge in this book, and another year writing it. I hope you found it valuable and full of ideas. And if it did indeed do that, I hope you'll find it in your heart to support me.

I assume many of you reading this are marketers, CMOs, and creators, so you know how important it is to support our community of marketers striving to do better. Below I'll list some ways that you can help support me and this book.

Review the book:

- Leave an honest rating (and some feedback!) on Amazon.
- Tweet me with your honest review (I can take it, I swear!)—@BrookeSellas.

Recommend the book:

- Send an email to your friends, coworkers, or boss and tell them why they should buy it.
- Buy a copy of the book for a friend, coworker, or your boss as a gift.
- Ask a team leader to consider the book for training; they can buy copies of the book for their entire team.

Shall we be social? Use #ThinkConversation to start the conversation!

- Share photos of you with your book, your highlighted notes, or your favorite quotes with the hashtag #ThinkConversation.
- Share a photo of you with your book on Instagram and tag me @brookesellas or B Squared Media @hellobsquared (and don't forget the #ThinkConversation hashtag).
- Tag me on Twitter and let's have our own conversation about the book.
- Post your endorsement of the book (with a photo, please!) on LinkedIn and be sure to tag me (Brooke Sellas—so far, I'm the only one I know of).
- You can post to Facebook, but since I don't use that platform personally, you're better off tagging B Squared Media, LLC (that goes for Facebook Groups, too!).

Connect me to yourself or others:

- Introduce yourself and your company if you think I can help you with anything mentioned in this book.
- Introduce me to friends, coworkers, or team leaders to recommend me for a workshop centered around social-led customer care or other areas mentioned in this book.
- Introduce me to event planners who are looking for speakers on any of the topics mentioned in this book.
- Introduce me to your own podcast or of someone you know so we can continue this very important conversation.

Join me on social for these and other conversations:

- Follow me on Twitter: @BrookeSellas. (I'm most active here!)
- Follow B Squared Media on Twitter: @HelloBSquared.
- Follow me on Instagram: @BrookeSellas. (Fair warning, it's a lot of horse mom stuff!)

- Follow B Squared Media on Instagram: @HelloBSquared.
- Connect with me on LinkedIn: https://www.linkedin.com/in/brookebsellas/.
- Follow the B Squared Media page on LinkedIn: https://www.linkedin.com/company/hellobsquared.

Notes

Introduction

1. "Meta Reports Fourth Quarter and Full Year 2021 Results," February 2, 2022, *Meta*, https://investor.fb.com/investor-news/press-release-details/2022/Meta-Reports-Fourth-Quarter-and-Full-Year-2021-Results/default.aspx.
2. Swetha Amaresan, "What Are Your Customers' Expectations for Social Media Response Time?," (blog), accessed November 16, 2021, https://blog.hubspot.com/service/social-media-response-time.

Chapter One

1. Anjali Lai, "Emotionally Charged Consumers are Ready for New Experiences," (blog) *Forrester*, July 1, 2021. https://www.forrester.com/blogs/emotionally-charged-consumers-are-ready-for-new-experiences/.
2. Lai, "Emotionally Charged Consumers are Ready for New Experiences."
3. Nidhi Arora, Daniel Ensslen, Lars Fiedler, Wei Wei Liu, Kelsey Robinson, Eli Stein, and Gustavo Schüler, "The Value of Getting Personalization Right—or Wrong—Is Multiplying," McKinsey & Company, November 12, 2021, https://www.mckinsey.com/business-functions/marketing-and-sales/our-insights/the-value-of-getting-personalization-right-or-wrong-is-multiplying.
4. B Squared Media, Based on data from Arora et al. "The Value of Getting Personalization Right—or Wrong—Is Multiplying."

Chapter Two

1. Irwin Altman and Dalmas A. Taylor, *Social Penetration: The Development of Interpersonal Relationships*, (New York: Holt, Rinehart and Winston, 1973).
2. Altman and Taylor, *Social Penetration*.
3. Ronald B. Adler, Russell F. Proctor II, and Neil Towne. *Looking Out, Looking In, 11th ed.* (Belmont, California: Wadsworth, 2005).
4. Altman and Taylor, *Social Penetration*.
5. Adler et al., *Looking Out, Looking In*.
6. Adler et al., *Looking Out, Looking In*.

7   Alvin Cooper and Leda Sportolari, "Romance in Cyberspace: Understanding Online Attraction." *Journal of Sex Education and Therapy* 22, no. 1 (June 1997): 7–14.
8   Jennifer Brooke Ballard, "An Evaluation Measuring the Patterns and Effects of Nonprofit Messaging Through Facebook," Thesis, (The Pennsylvania State University Brandywine, Spring 2011).
9   Proflowers (@ProFlowers), "This Is Your Reminder to Stop & Smell the Roses," Twitter, February 17, 2021, https://twitter.com/proflowers/status/1362163773918732290/photo/1.
10 United Airlines, "Weekly Deals from New York/Newark Under $120," Facebook, Accessed January 12, 2022, https://www.facebook.com/United/.
11 Proflowers (@Proflowers). 2022. "i can't and i won't slander carnations. They are gorg." Twitter, February 4, 2022, https://twitter.com/proflowers/status/1489694292734054413.
12 Sharpie (@Sharpie), "She met him at the office … He was bold and vibrant," Twitter, August 26, 2021, https://twitter.com/Sharpie/status/1430911504933588994.
13 Irwin Altman and Dalmas A. Taylor, "Communication in interpersonal relationships: Social penetration processes." In M. Roloff & G. Miller (Eds.), *Interpersonal Processes: New Directions in Communication Research*, (Newbury Park, CA: Sage, 1987), 257–277.

Chapter Three

1   James C. Collins, *Good to Great: Why Some Companies Make the Leap—and Others Don't*. 1st ed. (New York, NY: Harper Business, 2001).
2   "2021 Digital Experience Benchmarks/Compare Your Digital Performance," Contentsquare, accessed February 23, 2022, https://contentsquare.com/insights/digital-analytics-benchmarks/.

Chapter Four

1   Sprout Social, "Sprout Social Index™ Edition XVII: Accelerate," Accessed April 14, 2022, https://sproutsocial.com/insights/index/.
2   Jenna Chen, "Choosing the right social media channels for your business," (blog), *Sprout Social*, September 2, 2021. https://sproutsocial.com/insights/social-media-channels/.
3   Sprout Social, "Sprout Social Index™ Edition XVII: Accelerate."
4   Sprout Social, "#BrandsGetReal: What consumers want from brands in a divided society," (blog). Accessed November 16, 2021, https://sproutsocial.com/insights/data/social-media-connection/.
5   Fatemeh Khatibloo, Joanna O'Connell, and Tina Moffett, "Google Delays the Cookiepocalypse," *Forrester*, (blog), June 25, 2021, https://www.forrester.com/

Chapter Five

1. Evan Hamilton, email to author, February 23, 2022.
2. E. Hamilton, email.
3. Ross Quintana, email to author, February 21, 2022.
4. E. Hamilton, email.
5. *Oxford English Dictionary*, "Troll," Accessed March 29, 2022, https://www.oed.com/.
6. Hulk, Film Crit. Don't Feed the Trolls, and Other Hideous Lies." *The Verge*, July 12, 2018, https://www.theverge.com/2018/7/12/17561768/dont-feed-the-trolls-online-harassment-abuse.

Chapter Six

1. Christopher S. Penn, "Is Social Listening Useful?" (blog), Oct 21, 2021, https://www.christopherspenn.com/2021/10/is-social-listening-useful/.
2. Ballard, "An Evaluation Measuring the Patterns and Effects of Nonprofit Messaging Through Facebook."
3. Jeremy Linaburg (@jeremy_linaburg), "This is why @AppleMusic is the best! Just saying." Twitter, March 8, 2022, 2:01 p.m., https://twitter.com/jeremy_linaburg/status/1501271916501299202.
4. John D. Saunders (@johndsaunders), "I felt this, fr. I've been building mixes in Apple Music since 2015," Twitter, March 8, 2022, 11:14 p.m., https://twitter.com/johndsaunders/status/1501410960967450629.
5. Sephora (@sephora), "Mmmmmm … Check out this yummy, new collection of body products from @moroccanoil," Instagram photo, March 2, 2022. https://www.instagram.com/p/CanRP9fvco5/
6. Sephora (@sephora), "Picture of Ole Henriksen Strength Trainer Peptide Boost Moisturizer," Instagram photo, February 19, 2022, https://www.instagram.com/p/CaLCANsFqzG/.
7. Niki Hyde (@nikihyde). "Looking for some new social listening tools." Twitter, March 7, 2022, https://twitter.com/nikihyde/status/1500867594655576069.

Chapter Seven

1. Sprout Social, "Sprout Social Index™ Edition XVII: Accelerate."
2. Sprout Social, "Sprout Social Index™ Edition XVII: Accelerate."
3. Kristy Morrison, email to author, January 11, 2022.
4. James Avery Artisan Jewelry (@jamesavery), "We [heart] our home state! Celebrate #TexasIndependenceDay with some of our favorite designs," Instagram photo, March 2, 2022, https://www.instagram.com/p/Cam-nu0Bzax/.

5   Meta, "Bringing People Closer Together," *Meta*, January 12, 2018, https://about.fb.com/news/2018/01/news-feed-fyi-bringing-people-closer-together/.
6   Ernst Fehr and Simon Gächter. 2000. "Fairness and Retaliation: The Economics of Reciprocity." *Journal of Economic Perspectives*, 14 (3): 159–181.
7   Savannah Bee Company (@savannahbeeco), "Time for a Bee Fact! Did you know the average worker bee lives for just five to six weeks? During this time, she'll produce around a twelfth of a teaspoon of honey," Instagram photo, January 15, 2022, https://www.instagram.com/p/CYv_z_IMjHI/.
8   "LinkedIn Marketing Solutions on LinkedIn: Agree or Disagree: B2B Content Can Be Just as Fun as Consumer Content." Accessed March 16, 2022. https://www.linkedin.com/posts/linkedin-marketing-solutions_agree-or-disagree-b2b-content-can-be-just-activity-6888240845833818112-nWH6.
9   AQHA (@officialaqha), "Three-year-old Bruin Henry clambers into the truck beside his dad, Garrett," Instagram photo, Accessed March 15, 2022, https://www.instagram.com/p/CYsWQ_yAmgx/.
10 SmartPak (@smartpak), "Ever wondered what blanket might fit your horse best?," Instagram photo, January 16, 2022, https://www.instagram.com/p/CYz90s_tIIe/.
11 Walmart (@walmart), "What's Your Dad Story?", Instagram photo, August 16, 2021, https://www.instagram.com/p/CSo6rUdHTgV/.
12 Chick-Fil-A (@chickfila), "We're grateful for all who have sacrificed to protect our country." Instagram photo, May 31, 2021, https://www.instagram.com/p/CPixKF8s-8j/.
13 Duncan MacRae, "Three Quarters of Marketers Find B2B Engagement Harder than Ever," *Marketing Tech News*, January 11, 2022, https://marketingtechnews.net/news/2022/jan/11/three-quarters-of-marketers-find-b2b-engagement-harder-than-ever/.
14 LinkedIn Marketing Solutions, "'We've Reduced the Budget.' Name Another Marketing Four-Word Horror." LinkedIn, Accessed March 16, 2022, https://www.linkedin.com/posts/linkedin-marketing-solutions_weve-reduced-the-budget-name-another-activity-6894414969832648704-JYKG.
15 Julie Creswell, Kevin Draper, and Sapna Maheshwari. "Nike Nearly Dropped Colin Kaepernick Before Embracing Him." *The New York Times*, September 26, 2018, sec. Sports, https://www.nytimes.com/2018/09/26/sports/nike-colin-kaepernick.html.
16 Creswell et al., "Nike Nearly Dropped Colin Kaepernick Before Embracing Him."
17 Terence Smith, "Nike's Colin Kaepernick Ad Makes Sense After Looking at Customer Demographics," *The Inquisitr*, September 6, 2018, https://www.inquisitr.com/5059602/nikes-colin-kaepernick-ad-makes-sense-after-looking-at-customer-demographics/.
18 Ben & Jerry's (@benandjerrys), "Texas's New Abortion Law is Racist. Here's Why.," Instagram photo, September 29, 2021, https://www.instagram.com/p/CUa4sn1N5sl/.

19 Kim Severson, "Chick-fil-A's Many Controversies, Explained," *The New York Times*, July 26, 2012, sec. U.S. https://www.nytimes.com/2012/07/26/us/gay-rights-uproar-over-chick-fil-a-widens.html.
20 Gaby Del Valle, "Chick-Fil-A Has Long Had a Reputation for Anti-LGBTQ Donations. Now the Company Says That Will Change." *Vox*, November 19, 2019. https://www.vox.com/the-goods/2019/5/29/18644354/chick-fil-a-anti-gay-donations-homophobia-dan-cathy.
21 Sprout Social, "#BrandsGetReal: Brands Creating Change in the Conscious Consumer Era." Sprout Social. Accessed February 19, 2022, https://sproutsocial.com/insights/data/brands-creating-change/.
22 Jay Baer, "Why Broad Is Flawed in 2022 Marketing and Brand Positioning." Accessed February 23, 2022, https://www.linkedin.com/pulse/why-broad-flawed-2022-marketing-brand-positioning-jay-baer.
23 Accenture, "Life Reimagined: Mapping the motivations that matter for today's consumers," Accenture, Accessed March 10, 2022, https://www.accenture.com/us-en/insights/strategy/reimagined-consumer-expectations.
24 Patagonia, "Patagonia on LinkedIn, Patagonia Stopped All Paid Advertising on Facebook Platforms in June." LinkedIn, Accessed March 16, 2022, https://www.linkedin.com/posts/patagonia_2_patagoniastoppedall-paid advertising-on-activity-6859562936504070144-kCXb.
25 Sprout Social, "What Is Engagement Rate?", Accessed December 7, 2021, https://sproutsocial.com/glossary/engagement-rate/.
26 Sherwin-Williams, (@sherwinwilliams), "Get your paint on with one of our most popular (and versatile) colors ever, Iron Ore SW 7069.", Instagram photo, accessed March 15, 2022, https://www.instagram.com/p/CY5ASAJo9WA/.
27 Whataburger (@whataburger), "Quick question: Is it WHATAburger or WATERburger?" Twitter, February 12, 2021, https://twitter.com/whataburger/status/1360272848670056448?lang=en.
28 Blume (@Blume), Posted on Instagram: "You asked, we listened. A little birdie told us that a *lot* of you missed the dropper." Accessed March 15, 2022, https://www.instagram.com/p/CYrqyyGPkPo/.
29 Cloud Campaign, "How your agency team will feel after switching to Cloud Campaign," LinkedIn, Accessed January 18, 2022, https://www.linkedin.com/company/cloudcampaign/.
30 Mercer Smith, "111 Customer Service Statistics and Facts You Shouldn't Ignore," Help Scout, Accessed March 16, 2022, https://www.helpscout.com/75-customer-service-facts-quotes-statistics/
31 SnackMagic, "SnackMagic on LinkedIn: It's Really That Simple, Believe It or Not—With a Build-Your-Own Snack Spread," LinkedIn, Accessed March 16, 2022, https://www.linkedin.com/posts/snackmagic_its-really-that-simple-believe-activity-6888881509147774976-C9Xk..
32 Ecogold (@ecogold). Posted on Instagram: "When a piece of tack becomes a well-loved staple," Accessed March 15, 2022, https://www.instagram.com/p/CZAf7KOJURD/

Chapter Eight

1. Blake Morgan, "50 Stats That Prove the Value of Customer Experience," Forbes.com, Sep 24, 2019, https://www.forbes.com/sites/blakemorgan/2019/09/24/50-stats-that-prove-the-value-of-customer-experience/?sh=6cd152d24ef2.
2. Mark Schaefer, "The Aftermath of the Pandemic: How Customer Care Has Changed," (Webinar, B Squared Media, June 15, 2021), https://bsquared.media/webinars/pandemic-customer-care-webinar/.
3. Brandwatch, "Research: Do Brands Live Up to Customer Expectations on Social?" (blog), March 13, 2015, https://www.brandwatch.com/blog/research-do-brands-live-up-to-customer-expectations-on-social/.
4. Dale Carnegie, *How to Win Friends and Influence People: 30th anniversary edition* (New York: Simon and Schuster, 2009).
5. Vala Afshar, "New Rules of Customer Engagement: Key Findings from Global Research," Salesforce.com, Accessed January 11, 2022, https://www.salesforce.com/resources/articles/customer-engagement/.
6. Arora et al., "The Value of Getting Personalization Right—or Wrong—Is Multiplying."
7. "The Zendesk Customer Experience Trends Report 2020," (blog) Zendesk, December 26, 2019, https://www.zendesk.com/blog/zendesk-customer-experience-trends-report-2020/.
8. Reviewtrackers, "Online Reviews Statistics and Trends: A 2022 Report by reviewtrackers." Accessed December 30, 2021, https://www.reviewtrackers.com/reports/online-reviews-survey/.
9. Ian Jacobs and Kate Legget, "Win Funding For Your Customer Service Project." *Forrester*, August 14, 2020, https://www.forrester.com/report/Win-Funding-For-Your-Customer-Service-Project/RES82281.
10. Leslie Gaydos, "The Results Are in for Our Survey of Customer Service During COVID." NBC Boston (blog). Accessed February 16, 2022, https://www.nbcboston.com/investigations/consumer/nbc-boston-responds/the-results-are-in-for-our-survey-of-customer-service-during-covid/2233378/.
11. Ann-Marie Alcántara, "Customer Complaints, and Their Ways of Complaining, Are On the Rise." *Wall Street Journal*, June 15, 2020, sec. C Suite, https://www.wsj.com/articles/customer-complaints-and-their-ways-of-complaining-are-on-the-rise-11591998939.
12. Alcántara, "Customer Complaints."
13. B Squared Media, based on data from *NotifyVisitors*, "21+ Customer Experience Trends and CX Stats Brands Should Know." (blog), November 9, 2021, https://www.notifyvisitors.com/blog/customer-experience-trends/.
14. Baer, *Hug Your Haters*.
15. Baer, *Hug Your Haters*.
16. Sprout Social, "The Smart Inbox," Accessed March 4, 2022, https://sproutsocial.com/features/smart-inbox/.

Chapter Nine

1. Alex Debecker, "2022 Chatbot Statistics—All The Data You Need," (blog), Chatbot, August 23, 2017 (updated January 2022), https://blog.ubisend.com/optimise-chatbots/chatbot-statistics.
2. Debecker, "2022 Chatbot Statistics—All The Data You Need."
3. Sam Roverts, "Overlooked No More: Ruth Wakefield, Who Invented the Chocolate Chip Cookie," March 21, 2018, *The New York Times*, https://www.nytimes.com/2018/03/21/obituaries/overlooked-ruth-wakefield.html
4. Nestlé company website, Accessed March 15, 2022, https://cookiecoach.tollhouse.com/.
5. Edward O. Wilson, *Consilience: The Unity of Knowledge*, (New York: Random House 1999).
6. Patrick Bosek, "What Does It Mean to Manage Knowledge?" CMSWire, Simpler Media Group, Inc. January 12, 2022, https://www-cmswire-com.cdn.ampproject.org/c/s/www.cmswire.com/knowledge-findability/what-does-it-mean-to-manage-knowledge/amp/.

Chapter Ten

1. Linleigh Marie Kraft, email to author, May 23, 2022.
2. Kerastase (@KerastaseUSA), "I'm having problems checking out." Twitter, Accessed November 30, 2021, https://twitter.com/KerastaseUSA.
3. Diptyque (@diptyque), "Picture of Sapin candle," Instagram photo, December 22, 2021. https://www.instagram.com/p/CXzBxI1tD0l/.

Chapter Eleven

1. ResultsCX, "Consumer Appetite: Brand Inquiries via Social Media & Omnichannel," July 7, 2021, http://results-cx.com/press-release/resultscx-survey-illustrates-increased-consumer-appetite-for-resolving-brand-inquiries-via-social-media-omnichannel.
2. Amaresan, "What Are Your Customers' Expectations for Social Media Response Time?"
3. ResultsCX, "Consumer Appetite: Brand Inquiries via Social Media & Omnichannel."

Chapter Twelve

1. Small Business Administration, "How Much Does an Employee Cost You?" (blog) Accessed March 11, 2022, https://www.sba.gov/blog/how-much-does-employee-cost-you.

Chapter Thirteen

1. YouTube, "Home visit: transform a BILLY bookcase using fabric," IKEA channel, March 31, 2019. https://www.youtube.com/watch?v=4XoPLv5e-68&list=PLZKweYqjSlQSDvWFQVs7rniHlZPaXNYmE.
2. Salesforce.com, "State of the Connected Customer Report," 4th ed., Accessed February 16, 2022, https://www.salesforce.com/resources/research-reports/state-of-the-connected-customer/?d=cta-header-1.
3. Stephanie Stahl, "B2B Content Marketing Insights for 2022: More Budget, More Work, More Empathy," Content Marketing Institute. October 13, 2021, https://contentmarketinginstitute.com/2021/10/b2b-power-content-marketing-research/.
4. Drew Hansen, "Myth Busted: Steve Jobs Did Listen to Customers," *Forbes.com*, December 19, 2013, https://www.forbes.com/sites/drewhansen/2013/12/19/myth-busted-steve-jobs-did-listen-to-customers/?sh=18e5c23a87f3.

Index

A

Accenture, 113
account managers, 193
acquisition
   audience, 64
   automation, 156
   coding, 162, 163, 168, 171, 172
   conversations that connect, 124
   customer care, 131, 150
   digital customer journey, 49
   social media listening, 88
advocates
   as influencers, 90
   coding, 172
   customer care, 131, 133
   customer loyalty, 17
   customers, 64
   digital customer journey, 81
   metrics, 176, 184
   positive sentiment, 172
AI. *See* artificial intelligence
Alexa, 39, 166
Altman, Irwin, 21, 22, *23*
American Quarter Horse Association, 102, *103*
AMs. *See* account managers
Apple
   Apple Music, 82, 83
   community, 62, 202
   trolls, 67
AQHA. *See* American Quarter Horse Association
artificial intelligence, 151, 154, 155, 157
audience
   algorithms, 98
   American Quarter Horse Association, 102

   analysis, 89
   asking questions, 117
   breadth and depth, 117
   building, 94, 189
   coding, 162, 165
   communications, 77
   connections, 61
   consumer experience, 68
   conversations that connect, 99, 103
   COVID-19, 78
   customer loyalty, 135
   customers, 64
   digital customer journey, 81, 129
   digital customer journey flywheel, 39
   echoing, 78
   Ecogold, 125
   employees, 64
   engagement rates, 178
   feelings, 31
   finding, 82, 86
   followers, 64, 75
   Hamilton, Evan, 62
   identifying, 77
   in-house resources, 203
   lurkers, 69
   metrics, 177
   opinions, 31
   potholes, 127
   risk taking, 103, 108, 109, 110, 114
   seasonality, 190
   sentiment, 18
   social listening platforms, 79
   social media channel, 47
   social media intelligence, 53, 54
   social media listening, 71, 74, 80, 81, 89
   social penetration theory, 25, 26, 28, 29, 32, 34, 35, 36

surprise and delight, 96
tagging, 142
user-generated content, 105, 125
versus community, 63, 200
automation
   customer experience, 159

B

B2B. *See* business-to-business
Baby Boomers, 47
Baer, Jay
   broad is flawed, 113
   dissolution, 113
   Hug Your Haters, 112, 208
   reimagined customers, 113, 145
BCU, 143, 144, 145, 188, 190
Ben & Jerry's
   audience, 112
   broad is flawed, 113
   community, 111
   conversations that connect, 110
   feelings, 110
   opinions, 110, *111*
   risk taking, 112
   social media listening, 112
   versus Patagonia, 113, 115
Best Buy, 42
Beyoncé, 62
Black Lives Matter, 109, 110
Blume
   conversations that connect, 120
   feedback, 120, 146
   feelings, 120, 123
   opinions, 120, *121*, 123
   positive feedback, 191
   potholes, 127
Boolean, 88
bots. *See* chatbots
breadth
   audience, 28
   Baer, Jay, 113
   business-to-business, 102
   conversations that connect, 103
   definition, 22
   questions, 117
   social penetration theory, 32
B Squared Media
   empathy formula, 137

   flywheel, 37
   founding of, 6, 28
   identifying advocates and influencers, 172
   organizational structure, 192, 193
   professional provider, 188
   services, 208
   social-led customer care, 19, 134, 145
   social media platforms, 134
   stoplight system, 138
   teams not tech, 156
   teams, not tech, 158
   versus FTEs, 189
business-to-business
   audience, 102
   Cloud Campaign, 123
   conversations that connect, 105
   digital customer journey, 106
   LinkedIn Marketing Solutions, 106
   marketing, 105
   social-led customer care, 136

C

care squared training program, 202, 209
Carnegie, Dale, 134
cashback app, 145, 191
CEO. *See* chief executive officer
CFF. *See* Cystic Fibrosis Foundation
chatbots
   challenges, 155, 156, 158
   communication, 153
   cost-effectiveness, 153
   data, 157
   empathy, 155, 156
   response time, 153
   Ruth (Nestlé), 154
   social-led customer care, 151
Chewy, 95, *96*, 184
Chick-Fil-A
   audience, 105, 112
   community, 112
   conversations that connect, 127
   feedback, 112
   feelings, 105
   Instagram, *107*
   risk taking, 112
chief executive officer, 192

chief marketing officer
    Ben & Jerry's, 112
    building in-house, 192
    connecting with consumers, 15
    content budgets, 204
    potholes, 45
chief service officer, 192
clichés
    consumerism in crisis, 13
    content, 28, 99
    conversations that connect, 99, 127
    definition, 22
    nonprofit, 26
    ProFlowers, 29
Cloud Campaign, 121, *122*, 123
Clubhouse, 58
CMGRs. *See* community managers
CMO. *See* chief marketing officer
Coco the cat, 95, *96*
coffee filter anecdote, 157, 158, 168, 191
Collins, James (*Good to Great*), 37, 38
community
    audience, 62, 63, 64
    building, 5, 123, 125, 202
    coding, 161, 162, 174
    COVID-19, 15
    customers, 64, 68, 133
    Cystic Fibrosis Foundation, 5
    digital customer journey, 81
    digital customer journey flywheel, 38, 39, 40
    evangelism, 44
    Facebook, 6, 26
    feelings, 62, 105
    flywheel, *38*
    IKEA, 172, 202, *203*
    LGBTQ+, 112
    metrics, 184
    opinions, 62
    risk taking, 109, 114, 115
    social media intelligence, 57, 58
    social penetration theory, 21, 26
    user-generated content, 105
community managers
    conversations that connect, 124
    escalation of issues, 194
    social-led customer care, 134
    social media mystery shop, 201
    team skillsets, 195
consumer
    COVID-19, 16
    digital customer journey, 42
    emotions, 14, 15
    flywheel, 37
content marketing, 7, 77, 162
conversations that connect
    audience, 63
    automation, 156
    coding, 161, 174
    customer care, 129, 150
    social-led customer care, 136
    social penetration theory, 36
    team skillset, 194
    timing, 97
    user-generated content, 184
conversions, 58, 115, 132
Cookiepocalypse, 55, 56
Cooper, Alvin, 25
coronavirus. *See* COVID-19
COVID-19
    consumer behavior, 57
    consumerism in crisis, 13, 14, 15, 16
    online activity, 16
    online shopping, 56
    social-led customer care, 131
    social media listening, 78
CSO. *See* chief service officer
C-suite
    cost of social-led customer care, 151
    professional provider, 188
    testing digital customer journey, 49
customer-centric
    digital customer journey, 38, 40
    social-led customer care, 131, 133, 136
    social media intelligence, 57
    teams, 195
customer experience
    conversations, 16
    customer loyalty, 16, 64
    definition, 7
    digital customer journey, 37, 40, 42
    employees, 64
    ownership, 43
    personalization, 55, 56
    potholes, 45, 46
    retention, 43

social-led customer care, 129, 147, 151, 196
social media listening, 89
customer experience officer, 192
customer loyalty
  building, 17, 37
  customer care, 129
  customer experience, 16, 129
   digital customer journey stages, 43, 44
  social media intelligence, 56
customer support
  after hours, 7
  automation, 158
  brand reputation, 53
  coding, 162, 172
  cost savings, 132, 145
  customer care, 138
  definition, 133
  digital customer journey, 49
  documentation, 140
  in-house, 196, 197
  integration with other departments, 190
  loyalty, 149
  metrics, 177, 178, 181
  mystery shop, 196
  social media intelligence, 77
  team members, 193
  team skillset, 195
  tools, 151
  traditional structure, 133
  trolls, 68
  versus call center, 146
  versus customer care, 19, 39, 129, 181
CX. *See* customer experience
CXO. *See* customer experience officer
cystic fibrosis, 3, 4, 5
Cystic Fibrosis Foundation, 3, 5, 21

D

Dallas, 3, 4
DCJ. *See* digital customer journey
Deadmau5, 24
depth
  Baer, Jay, 113
  conversations that connect, 103
  definition, 22
  questions, 117
  social penetration theory, 22, 32

digital customer journey
  audience, 61
  automation, 156
  business-to-business, 106
  community, 63
  conversations that connect, 93, 125, 127
  digital touchpoints, 49
  potholes, 44, 45, 46
  social-led customer care, 129, 131, 132, 196
  social media intelligence, 51
  social media listening, 72, 78
  social penetration theory, 32
  stages, 40, *41*, 42, 48, 59
  surprise and delight, 95
  teams, 192, 196
digital customer journey flywheel
  community, 38, 40
  conversations that connect, 125
  customer care, *38*
  customer experience, 38
digital touchpoints
  definition, 46
  digital customer journey stages, 40
  identifying, 46
  improving digital customer journey, 196
  testing digital customer journey, 48
Diptyque, *170*
Discord, 74
dissolution
  Chick-Fil-A, 112
  definition, 35
  risk taking, 113
  social penetration theory, 25

E

Ecogold, 125, *127*
Eighth Semi-Annual Undergraduate Research at the Capitol, 26
empathy
  chatbots, 155, 156
  definition, 134, 136
  feelings, 137
  opinions, 137
  responding with, 137
  social-led customer care, 150
  social penetration theory, 24
  team skillsets, 195

trolls, 67
versus sympathy, 136
Emplifi, 185
employees
  audience, 64
evangelism, 43

F

Facebook
  algorithms, 98
  business pages, 4, 6
  Cystic Fibrosis Foundation, 21
  Cystic Fibrosis Foundation profile, 6
  digital customer journey, 40
  Patagonia, 114
  privacy settings, 81
  pub crawl, 20
  revenue, 6
  social media intelligence, 55
  social media listening, 74
  thesis, Ballard, 26, *27*
  United Airlines, *30*
  Young Professionals Leadership Committee, 4
facts
  Apple, 67
  audiences, 100
  community, 100
  conversations that connect, 99
  definition, 23
  examples, 24
  social media listening, 74
  versus opinions, 24
fandom
  community, 61, 62
  examples, 62
  Hamilton, Evan, 62
FAQ, 140, 141, 156
feedback
  coding, 174
  consumer use, 52
  digital customer journey, 46, 48
  frequency, 174
  negative, 18, 168
  social-led customer care, 191
  social media intelligence, 55
  social media listening, 89
feelings

conversations that connect, 99, 102, 105, 109
  definition, 24, 102
  LinkedIn Marketing Solutions, 106
  listening smart, 80
  questions, 117
  risk taking, 108, 109, 115
  Sharpie, 32
  social media listening, 80
  social penetration theory, 26, 31, 35
  trolls, 65
  user-generated content, 125
first touch resolution, 182
first touch response, 182, 183
first touch response time, 183
Floyd, George, 115
flywheel (Collins), 37, 38
Forrester Research, 14
freemium, 37
Friends (television show), 141
FTE. *See* full time employee
full time employee, 189, 190

G

Gen X, 52
Gen Z, 47, 52
Good to Great (Collins), 37
Google
  Google alerts, 185, 207
  Google My Business, 56, 207
  keywords, 86

H

Hamilton, Evan
  audience, 61, 62
  community, 63
  Reddit, 63
  social media channels, 62
Home Depot, 190
How to Win Friends and Influence People, 134
HubSpot, 179
Hug Your Haters (Baer), 113, 150, 208
Hunsaker, Lauren, 5
Hyde, Niki, *87*

I

IKEA, 171, 202

influencer marketing, 44, 73
influencers, 81, 90, 172
information technology, 131, 191
Instagram
    American Quarter Horse Association (AQHA), *103*
    Ben & Jerry's, *111*
    Chewy, 95
    Chick-Fil-A, *107*
    choosing your channels, 94
    Diptyque, *170*
    Ecogold, *127*
    James Avery Artisan Jewelry, *97*
    Moroccan Oil, *84*
    Sephora, 83, 84, *85*
    Sherwin-Williams, 47, *48*, *118*
    SmartPak, *104*
    Walmart, 105, *106*
IT. *See* information technology

J

James Avery Artisan Jewelry, 96, *97*
Jobs, Steve, 205

K

Kaepernick, Colin, 109, 110, 111
Kerastase
    feedback, 169
    Twitter, *169*
key performance indicator
    first touch response, 183
    identifying, 175
    potholes, 176
    response time, 180, 181
    teams, 192
keywords
    automation, 157
    Boolean searches, 88
    share of voice, 88
    social media listening, 85, 86, 87, 88
KPI. *See* key performance indicators
Kraft, Linleigh Marie, 163, 164

L

labeling. *See* tag
Letter, Jaime, 195
LGBTQ+ community, 112
Linaburg, Jeremy, *82*

LinkedIn
    book cover poll, 101
    Cloud Campaign, *122*
    Hootsuite, 121
    LinkedIn Marketing Solutions, *102*, *107*
    Patagonia, 113, *114*
    SnackMagic, *126*
    social media listening, 74
LinkedIn Marketing Solutions
    feelings, 102
    LinkedIn, *102*, 106, *107*
    opinions, 102
    polls, 102
Lowe's, 190
lurkers, 35, 68

M

Maine, 44
Marvel Entertainment, 62, 63
McKinsey & Company, 16, *17*, 135
Memorial Day, 105
mental retardation, 119
Mention (brand), 185, 207
mention (@mention)
    Apple Music, 83
    coding, 165, 166
    digital customer journey, 47
    keywords, 86, 88
    not tagged, 84
    responding, 85
    social media listening, 82
    Sprout Social, 86
    tag, 71
metrics
    choosing, 175
    coding, 174
    identifying, 175, 176
    negative sentiment, 183
    outbound volume, 177
    response and resolution, 182
    return on investment, 184
    tag, 162
    user-generated content, 184
Millennials, 52
Mister Rogers, 195
Moroccan Oil, 83
Morrison, Kristy, 95, *96*

Mother's Day, 116
MySpace, 4

N

National Bowling Association, 27
National Donut Day, 96
natural language processing, 166, 167
negative feedback, 143, 168
Negative Nancys, 146
Nestlé
    artificial intelligence, 154
    customer experience, 155
    Ruth (chatbot), 154, *155*
net promoter score, 183
New Jersey, 24, *30*
Nike
    audience, 109
    Black Lives Matter, 110
    community, 109, 110
    feelings, 110
    opinions, 110
    risk taking, 109, 110
    versus Ben & Jerry's, 111
NLP. *See* natural language processing
NPS. *See* net promoter score

O

Obama, Barack, 119
Ole Henriksen, *85*
    social media listening, 85
onion theory. *See* social penetration theory
opinion mining, 167
opinions
    book cover poll, 100, *101*
    by brands, 31
    conversations that connect, 99, 100, 101, 102, 109, 110
    definition, 24
    digital customer journey, 42
    Instagram, *121*
    news, 100
    political and social justice issues, 111, 112
    questions, 117
    risk taking, 108, 109, 115
    social media listening, 80
    social penetration theory, 26
    trolls, 65
    user-generated content, 125

P

pandemic. *See* COVID-19
Patagonia
    feelings, 115
    LinkedIn, *114*
    opinions, 113, 115
    risk taking, 113
PayPal, 176
Penn, Christopher, 73, 207, 208
Pennsylvania State Capitol, 26
Pennsylvania State University, The, 21, 26
personalization
    audience, 56
    automation, 156
    Cookepocalypse, 56
    customer loyalty, 135
    definition, 135
    Next in Personalization 2021 Report, 135
    revenue, 136
    social-led customer care, 132
platform is not the point, 58
PM. *See* project manager
polls
    book cover poll, 101
    choosing your channels, 94
    opinions, 100, 102
potholes
    automation, 157
    conversations that connect, 93, 127
    digital customer journey, 44
    metrics, 176, 183
    sentiment, 191
    social-led customer care, 145, 146, 149, 196
    social media intelligence, 58
Pride, 115
ProFlowers
    clichés, 28, *29*
    opinions, 31
    Twitter, *31*
project manager, 192, 195

Q

Quintana, Ross
    audience, 63

community, 63
Social Magnets, 63

R

Reddit, 63
reimagined customers
  Baer, Jay, 113, 145
  feelings, 113
  opinions, 113
reimagined customers, Baer, Jay, 113
reply time, 182
response rate, 182
response time
  automation, 153, 158
  B Squared Media, 19
  customer experience, 67, 180, 181
  goals, 176, 180
  metrics, 179, 181
  versus time to resolution, 182
return on investment, 156, 175, 184
Robbert, Katie, 208
ROI. *See* return on investment
Rosa's Law, 119
Ross Gellar, 141

S

sales-driven content
  feelings, 120
  opinions, 120
Sammons, Jill, 188, 190
Saunders, John D., *83*
Savannah Bee Company, 100
  feelings, 100
Schaefer, Mark, 131
seasonality, 190
self-disclosure, 21, 22, 28, 32, 34
Sellas, Alex, 192
sentiment
  coding, 161, 166, 173, 174
  definition, 167
  natural language processing, 166
  negative, 157, 168, 176, 183, 191
  neutral, 173
  positive, 167, 168, 171, 172, 191
  scores, 73, 143, 157, 166
sentiment analysis, 165, 167
  definition, 165
  influencers and advocates, 172

Sephora, 83, *84*, *85*
share of voice, 88, 89, 178
Sharpie, 32, *33*
Sherwin-Williams
  audience, 117
  audiences, 117
  digital customer journey, 47, *48*
  feelings, 117, *118*
  opinions, 117
  social penetration theory, 117
Sinatra, Frank, 24
Siri, 166
Slack, 74
SLPs. *See* social listening platforms
Small Business Association, 189
SmartPak
  customer support, 103
  feedback, 105
  feelings, 103
  Instagram, *104*
  user-generated content, 103
SnackMagic, 125, *126*
SnapChat, 58
social justice issues, 111
social-led customer care
  acquisition, 150
  automation, 153
  B Squared Media, 19
  building, 188
  coding, 162, 163, 164, 172, 177
  conversations that connect, 127
  cost, 189
  COVID-19, 131, 147
  customer experience, 129, 133, 196
  customer loyalty, 37, 129, 130
  definition of, 18, 130
  digital customer journey, 39, 40
  documentation, 138, 141, 142
  empathy, 137, 149
  feelings, 133
  flywheel, 38. *See* social-led customer care
  integration, 190
  key performance indicator, 181
  Negative Nancy, 143, 146
  personalization, 134
  professional provider, 187
  scaling, 189

seasonality, 95
social media listening, 88
teams, 39, 133, 190, 194, 196
triage, 138, 139, 141
versus traditional customer service, 133
social listening platforms, 72, 73, 78, 79, 175
Social Listening Step-By-Step (workbook), 82, 200, 208
social listening tools. *See* social media listening tools
Social Magnets, 63
social media. *See* social media channels; social media customer care; social media intelligence; social media listening; social media marketing; social media monitoring; social media platforms
audiences, 61
coding, 172, 174
communities, 21
digital customer journey, 42, 49
early beginning, 27
metrics, 178
social penetration theory, 25
team structure, 191
social media channels
algorithms, 98
challenges, 55
choosing, 94
coding, 161
digital customer journey, 47
metrics, 177
social-led customer care, 132, 133, 193
social media intelligence, 51, 56
social media customer care, 39, 130, 134
social media intelligence
cashback app anecdote, 145
challenges, 55
coding, 172
conversations, 145
Cookiepocalypse, 56
COVID-19, 57
definition, 18, 157
digital customer journey, 39, 47, 50, 93
increase in use, 56
metrics, 175
Negative Nancy, 143
Nike, 110

platforms, 58
social-led customer care, 130
social media listening, 78
third-party cookies, 56
social media listening
accuracy, 72
automation, 79
building in-house, 189, 193
coding, 161, 167, 172
consumer data, 72
COVID-19, 78
digital customer journey, 125
goals, 73, 82
investment, 78
keywords, 88
limitations, 73, 74
metrics, 185
negative sentiment, 120
opportunity, 71
quantifying results, 79
research, 72
sentiment, 143, 165
share of voice, 88
social media channels, 127
The Girl, 76, 77
thesis, Ballard, 79
The Woman, 77
versus social media monitoring, 71
social media listening tools, 185
coding, 166
data, 73
sentiment, 73
thesis, Ballard, 80
social media marketing, 61, 142
social media monitoring, 71, 200
social media mystery shop, 201, 209
social media platforms
choosing platforms, 101
demands, 18
social-led customer care, 134
social media listening, 86
team skillsets, 194
social penetration theory
algorithms, 98
balance of use, 106
basic principles, 36
brands and consumers, 36
breadth and depth, *23*

business to business, 105
companies, 25
conversations that connect, 36, 98
definition, 21
dissolution, 109
limitations, 35
online application, 25
online dating, 25
risk taking, 115
self-disclosure, 22
social-led customer care, 129
thesis, Ballard, 21, 26, 34, *108*
Special Olympics, 118
Sportolari, Leda, 25
Sprout Social
  consumers, 115
  consumer tastes, 112
  conversations that connect, 94
  description, 207
  Smart Inbox, 151, 185
  Social Listening Step-By-Step (workbook), 200, 208
  social listening tools, 86
  social media intelligence, *52, 53, 54*
stoplight system, 139, **140**
stories
  American Quarter Horse Association, 102
  audiences, 116
  feelings, 116
  marketing, 14
  opinions, 116
  social penetration theory, 34
surprise and delight, 184
Swift, Taylor, 62

T

tag
  acquisitions, 162, 163
  coding, 164, 165
  digital customer journey, 47
  empathy, 161
  feedback, 89, 165
  feelings, 161, 166
  incorrectly, 84
  metrics, 162, 178
  negative sentiment, 143
  not tagged, 83, 86
  opinions, 161, 166
  sentiment, 173, 183
  social media intelligence, 161
  social media listening, 80
  social media listening tools, 162
  surprise and delight, 184
  thesis, Ballard, 79
tagged. *See* tag
tagging. *See* tag
Talkwalker, 185, 207
Tassopoulos, Tim, 112
Taylor, Dalmas, 21, 22, *23*
teams, not tech, 158, 167
Texas, 24
  James Avery, 96
  Texas Independence Day, 97
  Whataburger, 119, 120
The Girl (jewelry brand example), 74, 75, 76, 77
The Woman (jewelry brand example), 77
Think Conversation, Not Campaign, 26, 27, 28, 87
TikTok, 58, 74
time to resolution, 147, 182, 183
trolls
  audience, 68
  feelings, 68
  opinions, 68
  policy, 67
Trust Insights, 73, 207, 208
Twitter
  Apple Music, *82, 83*
  choosing your channels, 94
  Hyde, Niki, *87*
  Kerastase, *169*
  ProFlowers, *29, 31*
  red flag cliché, 100
  Sharpie, *33*
  social media intelligence, 55
  social media listening tools, 73
  Whataburger, *119*

U

ubisend, 153
UGC. *See* user-generated content
United Airlines, *29, 30*
user-generated content
  conversations that connect, 125

Ecogold, 125
  identifying, 125
  IKEA, *203*
  metrics, 184, 185
  positive sentiment, 171
  SmartPak, 103, 105
  surprise and delight, 184

V
Verge, 65

W
Wakefield, Ruth, 155
Wall Street Journal, 148
Walmart
  audience, 105
  feelings, 105
  Instagram, *106*
  opinions, 105
  versus Chick-Fil-A, 105
  web3, 62
Whataburger
  audience, 119, 120
  conversations that connect, 119
  feelings, 127
  opinions, *119*, 120, 127
  poll, 127
Wilson, E.O., 157

Y
Young Professionals Leadership Committee, 3, 4, 5
YouTube, 110, 191, *203*
YPLC. *See* Young Professionals Leadership Committee

About the Author

Brooke B. Sellas has more than fifteen years of experience in digital marketing, with an expertise in social media marketing. After an early career in real estate, Brooke became dedicated to raising awareness of cystic fibrosis, a disease that impacts more than 30,000 Americans (including her sister). She served as director of special events for the Cystic Fibrosis Foundation for several years. She founded B Squared Media in 2012, based on her marketing mantra: Think Conversation, Not Campaign™. Since then, Brooke and the B² Crew have become known as the "conversation company" with their done-for-you social media, advertising, and online customer care solutions that focus on customer-centric strategies. Clients include billion-dollar brands, not-for-profits, and small-to-medium enterprises.

In addition to her client services, Brooke is a guest speaker at major marketing venues across the country, including Social Media Marketing World, Agents of Change, and Content Jam. She also has taught social media studies at New York University, Baruch College, and the University of California at Irvine. Brooke holds a degree in communications from The Pennsylvania State University.

When Brooke isn't helping create conversations that connect, she can be found in a New Jersey pasture with her quarter horse, Diva, or searching for real Tex-Mex along the Eastern seaboard. She lives in New Jersey with her husband, Alex.

Made in the USA
Monee, IL
27 September 2023

43520968R00146